AMERICA 3:16

AMERICA
3:16

FAMILY, FAITH, FREEDOM...FOREVER!

GRAHAM ALLEN

FREEDOM IMPRINT

AMERICA 3:16

Family, Faith, Freedom, Forever

ISBN   978-1-5445-0869-6 *Hardcover*

   978-1-5445-0868-9 *Ebook*

   978-1-5445-0870-2 *Audiobook*

To my amazing wife, Ellisa: you hold my entire heart! Thank you for sticking with me when I didn't even know who I was. Thank you for seeing me not for who I was, but for who I could be. Most of all, and I do mean most of all, thank you for choosing me!

To my beautiful children, thank you for giving me the greatest gift of all. I get to be your dad!

To Gage, thank you for teaching me what it means to be a parent. Your heart is so big and I am in awe of you every single day. We grew up together, kiddo, and I owe you so much for teaching me what it means to be a man.

To Gunnar, thank you for showing me what it means to take life as it comes to you. I have never met a young man who takes what is given and makes it the best situation possible, like you do every single time. You and your brother will be amazing leaders one day, and I look forward to seeing it.

To AnnaGrace, thank you for showing me that we have so much love in our hearts to give. Just when I thought I couldn't possibly love any more you came along and wrapped me around your finger. Thank you for showing me the amazing gift of having a daughter. You are my best girl, and I cannot wait to see the woman you become.

Also, if we happen to be blessed enough to add to our family—I love you too!

I hope one day you all will be able to look back on this book and know more of who your dad was as a person, flaws and all.

To my parents, thank you for the gift of life. Thank you for your roles that you played in my life. They weren't all good, but they weren't all bad. To my dad, I love you and I am glad you are a part of my life. To my mom, I still love you, and I hope you find the peace you are looking for one day.

To my Maw and Paw, thank you for being there for me when no one else was. Thank you for taking the burden of raising me when you didn't have to. Thank you for teaching me that life was possible outside of my struggle. Thank you for teaching me when the world just wanted to push me aside. Thank you for being my parents when I needed parents the most. Thank you for never giving up on me even when you probably should have. Thank you for loving me.

To all of my friends who are family: How crazy has this ride been? Thank you for being the missing pieces in my life that I needed for so long. Thank you for showing me the best parts of the world when I had nothing but hurt to compare it to. Thank you for being my family.

And last but never least, to John, Chris, and Chausse: I wish you guys were here to see this! I hope I am making you proud. I know you are all looking down on me, so I just want to say one thing: Thanks for believing in me!

CONTENTS

FAMILY

INTRODUCTION..11

1. EVERY STORY HAS A BEGINNING....................... 15

2. EVERY BEGINNING HAS AN END.................................. 45

3. NOT YOUR AVERAGE WAR STORY............................. 65

4. HOW I MET YOUR MOTHER...................................... 97

5. THE DAILY RANTS 117

FAITH

6. TOXIC MASCULINITY 149

7. TATTOOS 167

8. CONSERVATIVES CAN'T BE CHRISTIANS?.................189

FREEDOM

9. PATRIOTISM IS *NOT* RACISM....................................199

10. LIFE STARTS NOW 207

11. DO YOU KNOW WHERE YOUR KIDS ARE? 217

12. GUN RIGHTS ARE HUMAN RIGHTS............................ 227

FOREVER

13. OUR RIGHTS AND OUR FREEDOMS ARE
    NOT UP FOR DEBATE...239

ABOUT THE AUTHOR...247

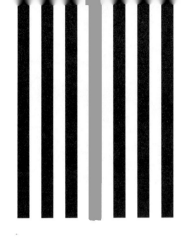

FAMILY

If there is one thing that grounds me, it is my family. I believe that deep down we all want to obtain a better life and pass that better life on to our own personal version of the next generation. I believe that one of the greatest things we can ever do is to show the world what we believe by practicing what we preach within our own homes. Family is the one thing that proves to us how lucky we are every single day. Good or bad, family defines us. Family centers us and sends us on our path.

INTRODUCTION

DEAR AMERICA

What if I told you a story? Would you listen? What if I wrote you a story? Would you read it? What if I told you we are all the same? Would you accept it?

What if I told you that life is an amazing place, and that war and hatred among people, genders, and religions didn't exist? Imagine a place where you can get whatever you want. Every dream you've ever thought possible can come true. You never get tired. You're never hated. Everyone loves you for your beliefs and values. You never have to worry about bills or your kids growing up to be good people or who to vote for or whether your spouse is being faithful to you.

Would you believe me?

I didn't think so.

What if I told you that people reflect the love of the Creator they claim to believe? What if I said everyone lived together differently and in their own way, but as one people: Americans.

Would you believe me?

If you're looking for a book to provide the answer to all of society's problems, I'm afraid this isn't the book for you. If you're looking for a book that makes you feel like the world is a safe space for everybody and that life is great, this isn't the book for you either. Maybe try a romance novel or a story where the reluctant hero emerges victorious in the end (I recommend *To Kill a Mockingbird* or *Pride and Prejudice*.) If you're looking for an escape from the real world, this is your chance to walk away now.

If you're still here, you might be wondering why the author of a book would tell you to stop reading. The answer is simple.

The purpose of this book is to tell you *what you need to hear*, not what you want to hear.

You may think you know me. You may think you don't agree with me—or that you do. You may be surprised if you keep reading.

I divided this book into four sections. The first three—Family, Faith, Freedom—reflect my core principles. If you want to understand why I stand where I do on certain issues, you have to know where I come from and what I have experienced.

In the Family section, I share my family experiences, good and bad, that have shaped my beliefs.

In the Faith section, I describe how my Christian beliefs were formed through my childhood, adolescence, deployments, and marriage.

In the Freedom section, you'll read the behind-the-scenes stories of some of the most impactful videos, rants, and newsworthy events I have made, and understand where they came from.

The fourth section—Forever—is a call to action. Will you answer it?

Think of this as a love-hate situation. You may love what you read here; you may hate what you read here. But that's a choice. Reading this book is a choice which you should make. What I have to say should not be forced on anyone. As a reader, you always have a choice. By its very definition, a choice means freedom. I'm offering you the freedom to walk away now.

Are you still here? Good.

Let's get started.

CHAPTER 1

≡

EVERY STORY HAS A BEGINNING

"I know you're going to Hell, and we tried everything to save you. Good riddance."

—MY STEPFATHER

DISCLAIMER: Throughout this story I reveal details of my life that no one has ever heard or read before. I talk about the people within it, both good and bad, who shaped me into who I am. To protect and secure their privacy and safety, their names have been changed.

I suppose it makes the most sense for you to know the story of the person who is writing this book. I suppose that will add perspective to the man who you think you know from TV, the internet, or simply by hearing my voice. I honestly never imagined writing about myself would be so difficult, even though I have heard from many others that talking about ourselves is often the hardest thing to do.

You see, it's easy to learn and to educate yourself about something you are interested in. You *choose* to learn and to have an opinion on things because they mean something to you. Yet your life is not something any of us get to choose. Well, at least not the beginning.

I wrote this book to give you context as to who I am. First and foremost, I am a Christian. I promise that once you hear my story—my full story—you will marvel as I do at the crazy ways God works, and how everything makes sense in the end. I wrote this book not only to share my thoughts on politics, culture, and religion within our nation; I also wrote it to speak to the very people who can relate to it in their own way. Maybe that means you. We all have a past. This is mine.

CALEDONIA, MISSISSIPPI

The beginning—where to even start? Let me ask you this: What is your first memory as a child? I want you to think really hard. Do you have it? What is it? Is it a nice memory? Maybe a trip to the park, or getting your favorite ice cream? Maybe it's a person comforting you, or a time when you felt truly free, without a care in the world?

My very first memory is being lost—it's amazing how a twelve-hundred-square-foot house can seem so large when you are so very young. I couldn't find my parents anywhere in our house in Caledonia, Mississippi.

So my first memory is of intense fear. I was terrified by their absence. I remember running, screaming, and banging on neighbors' doors.

Thankfully, the nice lady next door helped me find them; turns out they had been in the laundry room the whole time.

Fear was an uncommon feeling in my early childhood—that's probably why I remember it. But fear was going to become a big part of my life as I grew older, and that fear grew out of what my home life eventually would become.

I want to begin by telling you where I'm from. I have a feeling that if you understand that, it will bring some clarity on why I feel the way I feel about so many things.

"Mississippi is an all right place to be born," my grandfather used to tell me, "but you'll probably never want to visit." I never really understood what he meant until I got older. Mississippi was all I knew, and it was my home. I was born in Biloxi, on the coastline of Mississippi made famous by Hurricane Katrina. Very early on, my parents moved up to Northeast Mississippi, to a small town called Caledonia. There wasn't much in Caledonia then, and honestly there still isn't. The population to this day is about 1,100 people within city limits. We have one flashing traffic light, and our claim to fame is that the late, great Elvis Presley was born forty-five minutes north in Tupelo. I will say that they have really blown up over the past thirty years and have recently added a Dollar General as the main attraction for potential movers into the community.

Caledonia is located halfway between Mississippi State University and University of Alabama. My mother's family were Mississippi State fans; my father's lived and died by Alabama. Early in life I decided to Roll with the Tide, and I've been wearing an Alabama hat ever since.

My town felt like Mayberry, USA. One day, we couldn't get where we needed to go because the local cows had gotten out and blocked the only road (my friends and I used to mark the cows with paint-ball guns—if you saw one with a blue splotch, you knew Graham Allen had been there). When a new gas station came to town, it was such a big event that the local radio station covered it and the mayor opened the new store with a ribbon cutting ceremony. That's right, we had a ceremony for the opening of a gas station. If you wanted to see the rest of the world, the only ways out were community college or joining the military.

I grew up in this small-town way of life, where seeing New York City was on people's bucket list, something that they may or may not actually accomplish. I didn't realize it then, but I realize it now—Caledonia was special. It was a town that time truly had forgotten. It was a place where your kids could ride up and down the road and not come back until dark. In fact, I remember many days my grandparents telling me I couldn't come back inside until dark. Today that would be considered "child abuse." Caledonia was a place where most people didn't even lock their doors. It was a place that taught me how to be who I am. You see, people from Caledonia don't care about what you have or what you don't. They care about your character. They care about what really matters. It's not about what you achieve in this life that counts. It's what you do to affect people's lives in a positive way that means more than money, fame, or status ever could.

I wasn't anything special growing up. I was an awkward kid. I was skinny. I was short. I wasn't athletic by nature. In fact, I learned very early in life how horribly cruel my classmates could be even in elementary school because I looked a little different than they did.

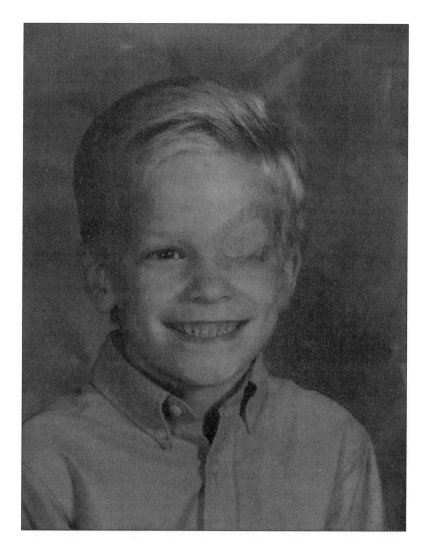

You see, I had a little bit of a vision problem. I had a lazy eye, so very early on the doctors made me wear an eye patch to strengthen the weak eye. I heard everything under the sun: Graham Cracker, Golden Graham, Graham Maw, Graham Paw, Grahama Lama Ding Dong, and the list goes on and on. My favorite was Three Eyes. I must admit, that one was clever. Four eyes is what you call kids who wear glasses. Because I wore glasses and an eye patch, they simply took a number away. Like I said, pretty clever. (This picked-on kid would go on to be heard and seen by billions, but we aren't at that part of the book yet.)

My mom was twenty-five, and my dad was twenty-seven when they had me. By the time I was seven years old they had divorced twice and remarried once. In the end, my parents weren't just divorced—they hated each other, on both sides. I was born into a broken environment; I was a national statistic. I lived the reality of broken families that is one of the biggest issues in our society—something I'll write more about later in this book.

I preface these next few paragraphs by saying this: my dad and I have a good relationship now, and he is known as PawPaw to my kids. However, we are not talking about right now; we are talking about the past. Looking back as an adult, I can see my dad was just an irresponsible kid who wasn't ready to have a kid himself. His father died when he was a teenager, and to say he never recovered from that would be an understatement. He never regained his footing after losing his father.

I idolized my dad.

Like most sons, I thought he was Superman and the coolest person on the planet. Yet, he was a hothead, always one step away from trouble—or actually stepping right into it. My dad's record isn't what you would call spotless. In fact, I didn't know it at the time, but just about every single person my dad knew or was friends with had drug or legal problems. My dad had his share of trouble with the police, and his life choices would lead to needing a liver transplant later in life. (He's alive today thanks to that transplant.)

The car business runs in my family. Dad has always been in the body shop world, and the rest of his family have worked as car salesmen. I guess I get my ability to talk for a living genetically. My mom was a chemistry teacher for much of my childhood. She prided herself on being the smartest person in any room she walked into. The worst part about that statement is more often than not, she was.

My dad and I have a good relationship now, but the past is what it is, so we need to address it. Before we settled in Caledonia, we moved all over Mississippi. It is sad to say, but I remember a time when I was eight, and we were living in Gulfport, that my mom locked herself into a room with me. I remember my dad yelling and banging on the other side of the door. I remember screaming and crying and my mom pleading for my dad to stop. To this day, I have no idea what this particular argument was about. I just added it to the list of many. It wasn't uncommon for my mom and dad to be at each other's throats about something. My dad seemed like a terrible person at the time, thanks to my mother drilling into my head every single day just how bad he was. Later on in life, I would come to find out that my mother was no saint in their relationship, either. All I know is in that exact moment I was terrified of my own father.

By the time I was eight my parents had divorced for good, and my mom wanted my dad to stay as far away as possible. Imagine "the absolute worst human being alive." That is how my mother would describe my father to me on a daily basis. In all fairness, he didn't do anything during this time period to really prove her wrong, either. When he did come around, people confronted him to keep him away from us. One time my grandfather actually headbutted him in the front yard.

Today, my dad knows he was crazy at that time period in his life. We have talked about that particular moment a hundred times over the years. Another time, he came to the Baptist church Mom and I were attending in Columbus. The pastor confronted him in the parking lot while we hid in his house next door. Pastor Chuck was a little guy, but he wasn't going to let my dad get to me and my mom. It is hard to say exactly how I felt. After all, I was just a kid, the same age that my oldest son is now. As a father, I find it insane to realize that my son will forever remember what I do as his dad. Much like I will always remember my parents. I guess the moral to that story is…be careful, because one day your kid may just write a book.

In the early days after the divorce, it was my mom and me against the world.

I didn't understand why people thought my dad was horrible, but they certainly told me he was horrible. After he left, my mom and I moved in with her parents, Alan and Rose Whistler. No one called them that, though. To the entire neighborhood they were affectionately known as Maw and Paw.

At the time, I didn't think there was anything strange about living with my grandparents. That's just the way things were. From that moment, my grandparents became the most reliable and trustworthy parental figures in my life. To this day, I still think of them as my parents. The truth is, I needed them. I had so much self-doubt as a child that I needed something stable in my life. They were not perfect, just as none of us are. Yet they loved me and stepped in when they didn't have to.

My grandfather has always been full of sayings that oftentimes came off as riddles, although I'm not sure he meant them to. "Graham," he would tell me, "I don't care if you are ugly as a mule or as dumb as an ox, as long as you are good!" I never was quite sure what he was trying to tell me. Was he trying to break it to me that I was going to have a hard time finding a date? Was he telling me that I better learn a life skill because book smarts weren't my thing? Who knows honestly? Another thing I heard a lot was, "Graham, you are 80 percent there!" Except the percentage would change constantly. The next time he saw me he would say, "Graham, you are 75 percent there!"

I was left to wonder what I'd done to drop 5 percent. Did I make a huge life mistake? Or was it a simple old man slip and he just forgot what he said last time? I guess only Paw knows that one. I suppose I was looking for approval in those early years. It certainly didn't come easy. My entire early childhood felt like purgatory to what would eventually be: my mom and me against the world. My dad as the villain. My grandparents as the wise figures who would step in where others had failed. It was a life, and I can say I had it worse than others and better than some. Yet, even at a young age, I felt like this couldn't be all of it.

THE STEPDAD

When Pastor Chuck and his family left our church for another congregation, my mom and I switched churches, too. We joined the First Assembly of God Church in Columbus, about fifteen miles away. There, my mom met a guy. It felt to me like they dated forever, because I was a kid and didn't have a good sense of time in general. In reality, everything happened pretty fast. One minute, I was living with my grandparents. The next minute, Mom and I had moved into an apartment with my new stepdad and his two daughters from a previous marriage who would visit once or twice a month.

They actually lived with their mother. I suppose this should have been a warning sign of things to come. Yet, as usual, I was told that my stepfather's ex was the devil, that she did him terribly wrong. I mean, she took his daughters away, and found another man blah blah blah! As adults, my younger stepsister and I still are in touch periodically. We don't speak about my stepdad or my mother much; it is a trauma that none of us want to revisit. Looking back, the beginning of my time with him seems like the early scenes of a suspense thriller, with the new stepdad who seems so nice. I believed in this new family. I trusted that this was going to be a good thing, but it wasn't.

Here's the thing: This is a hard chapter for me to write. It may turn out to be a hard chapter for you to read. I know people had it worse than me when they were growing up, but I didn't have it easy. Today, I actually don't blame my parents, even though that's a popular thing to do in our culture. In fact, I understand that my father never recovered from his father's death, and I know that my mother struggled with mental illness. I'm not here to blame anybody. Look at it this way: If I'd had a perfect childhood, I probably never would have created The Daily Rants and experienced all the amazing success that has come from that. I never would have made the decisions that led me to the corner of Pearman Dairy Road in Anderson, South Carolina where I made my first video. I would have never met my beautiful wife and had my amazing children. Also, it's safe to say I wouldn't be writing this book and you wouldn't be reading it.

Even when things were darkest, I know now that God was working in my life. I may not have realized it then, but I can look back and see His hand at work. You may not realize it in your own life, but no matter how dark things are now, there is always a tomorrow, and God is working in your life. In fact, I've learned that it is when we think God isn't there that He is actually working the hardest behind the scenes, lining up what He has in store for us next!

I faced what I faced, and I'm here to tell you about it. Not to lay blame, but to lay out the facts and what it was like for me.

SWEET CAROLINE

My stepdad came from a super religious, Old Testament style, works-driven background. From his point of view, if he wasn't moving forward, he was backsliding. That became an important concept in my life: *backsliding.* Now that I was part of his family, I discovered that these principles applied to me, too. When we moved into his apartment, I encountered many, many rules I'd never heard before. In his eyes, I was backsliding pretty much all the time. I had been saved by Jesus at a young age, but in his biblical worldview, that wasn't good enough. I had to be saved constantly! I am not saying that rules and discipline are not important. In fact, I believe in them wholeheartedly. However, this was different. This was something else. There was a darkness in this place, a heaviness that I couldn't understand then, but that I was about to live. I was about to live it every single day for years.

When I compare my stepdad's approach with the one I take today, I know how different my sense of God and religion is. But as a child, I didn't understand that there could be a different way.

When I was in third grade, my mom became pregnant. A new sister was on the way and Caroline was going to be her name. About five months into the pregnancy, though, Mom and my stepdad moved to the Ronald McDonald House in Jackson, Mississippi. I didn't know it at the time, but that's where parents who have children with serious health issues go when they can't afford anyplace else.

Caroline was born three months prematurely. In third grade, I traveled back and forth to Jackson with Maw to visit. It felt like I barely attended school, I spent so much time there. I wasn't allowed in the room to touch Caroline. I could only see my sister through the glass, in an incubator. I remember listening to a Petra song, *Beyond Belief*, on the drives back and forth. I liked rock music, and Petra made the Stepdad Approved/Acceptable List of allowable music. I thought to myself, "God has this. It's going to be okay."

Unfortunately, Caroline didn't make it. It was the 90s, after all, and medical treatments and advances weren't what they are today. That moment marked my first questioning of how real God actually was. Why did my sister die? Why do bad things happen to good people? It's the question that most people are faced with in their lives, and I wasn't prepared to answer it as a third grader.

A few days after she died, I went with my stepdad to buy Caroline's tombstone, and I finally saw what appeared to be a normal emotion come from him. He made me wait in the car, but through the glass of the storefront, I watched him cry.

The one and only time I got to hold my sister was after she'd died. For the first and last time, I held her outside that clear box, without the tubes and wires that she'd always been attached to. I was too young to really process my feelings, but I do remember that life didn't seem real, somehow. I was torn up inside, and I was crying on the outside. Strangely, I noticed my mother wasn't. I didn't know how to grieve, and I ended up withdrawing into myself. Caroline's death was a devastating blow for our family. The larger tragedy, for me, came later. As an adult now, I realize that my firm stance on when a life is a life started at this moment. Caroline was so small. Yet, she was a person, and she had such a huge impact on me. She was taken so soon. Yet, she mattered to so many. She was a person, and I still think of her to this day.

The damage that I didn't see at the time was about to come full circle in front of me. Caroline's death took my mom away from me. She was so calm after Caroline died, and I thought, shouldn't she be more upset? The truth is, I never really saw my mother again after that day. The person who had been my mother went somewhere else that day, and I never got her back after that.

The hardest part about my history with my mother is I believe she loved me and still does. I really do believe she only wanted what was best for me. But Caroline's death broke something in my mom. Up until that point, she had been my biggest advocate. I had been trying to learn how to live this new life with my stepdad, and my mom went to bat for me in this new family. That person, however, was no longer there. The next six years would become a seemingly endless journey for her and me of pain, hurt, and emotional struggle that cost us our relationship. What do you do when your rock-laid foundation crumbles? What do you do when your best friend goes away? Most of all, what do you do when you find yourself alone? Most people respond in different ways. This is my version.

After Caroline died, my mom stopped pushing back against my stepfather and his "new world order" for our blended family. Religion was his life, religion was everything, and now religion was our law. I was just a kid trying to figure out how to fit in and get by. Yet, I learned very quickly with no one to run interference for me anymore that my life was about to take turns that I never expected.

My mom's health started to decline dramatically. She experienced depression and other mental health issues. Once I started fifth grade, she stopped working and became dependent on medications, particularly for ADD and depression. She also suffered from frequent migraine headaches. She relied on support from the government to get by, and always seemed to see things happening around her in the darkest terms.

During this time, my stepdad was injured while working at Weyerhaeuser. He recovered, but never went back to work. Like my mom, he ended up addicted to ADD medication, and he too suffered from constant migraines. They always seemed to be in bed or lying on the couch with something covering their eyes. Neither of them was very functional.

I know now that my mom suffered, and suffers, from real mental health issues. I didn't know that then. I simply knew that things had changed for the worse. In fact, that change was only the beginning.

My life was about to get a *lot* worse.

THE HOMESCHOOL YEARS

Have you ever felt like you couldn't do anything right? Well, that was my daily burden as I tried to understand why my parents were always upset about everything I did. I either wasn't smart enough or "Christian" enough to gain their approval. My stepdad was never happy about anything—in fact, he was always one step away from being furious about everything.

One Christmas, he let me know how much he hated the post office. Workers at the local post office would write back to kids who had sent letters to Santa. He was angry because he knew the post office (as Santa) would tell me I was a good boy when *obviously* I was terrible and deserved nothing for Christmas. This is also how I found out that Santa wasn't real—because he was attempting to prove to me how bad I was.

The worst part of this is, I was not a bad kid. You may be thinking,

"Sure, that's what *all* bad kids say," but when I look back now, I see that I was actually a pretty good kid. Was I perfect? Absolutely not! However, I tried hard, but I never seemed to be good enough—so I *thought* I was the worst kid in the world, because that's what I heard every day. That's *all* I heard every single day.

Up through fifth grade, I went to a Christian school. Obviously, when you have the most "Christian" parents on the planet, you go to a Christian school. I met a girl there named Ellisa. (Spoiler alert: Many years later I am blessed enough to call her my wife, but that comes later in the story. I told you God was constantly working in my life.) My mother was an academic, and she decided that any grade less than an A was unacceptable—and "unacceptable" equaled punishment. My teachers were under strict orders to contact my parents if I didn't perform to my mother's standards. It's one thing to know you have let your parents down and there will be consequences. It's another to know there is no way to win, and that no matter what you do, you are doomed. That's how my life felt.

By sixth grade, both Mom and my stepdad were at home 24/7. That's when they decided to focus their full attention on me. They concluded that my school just was not making me a good enough person. They wanted to ensure that the only voices I heard were the ones they wanted me to hear—theirs. And so the homeschooling era began. In this arrangement, my mom was the teacher and my stepdad was the enforcer. Lord knows they had their share of demons, and they took them out on me whenever they had the chance.

I hated every second of it.

Nowadays, homeschooled kids are encouraged to go through the academic curriculum and also to engage in social activity with other kids. My experience was the opposite.

My transition to homeschooling led to total isolation from the outside world. Here's one example of what that meant: A church sat across the road from our house in Caledonia. It had a basketball court, which I could see from my room. I remember watching kids play basketball every day. My town only had 1,100 people, yet I didn't know a *single one* of those kids! I so badly wanted to go play with them, but I wasn't allowed to. I was so alone. I was a middle school kid who was literally under house arrest.

I don't remember much from that year, except that it seemed to be one, gigantic "lesson." I *do* remember being up at 2 a.m. trying to pass a math test my stepdad had given me. When I gave it to him he would work the problems, tell me it wasn't right, and hand the test back—but not actually *teach* me anything. I would go back to my desk and do them all again. This happened again and again, until I passed most nights around midnight. I began to grow nauseous over taking tests.

Because my parents were always sick, or seemed to be, I spent a lot of time alone. Like most kids that are alone, the only friends I had were imaginary ones.

In sixth grade, I began to struggle with depression. I developed anxiety related to hypochondria. As I watched my mom getting sicker and sicker, I thought it was only a matter of time before the same thing happened to me. I would feel the different parts of my body, looking for indications that I was ill. If I found something suspicious, I would tell myself, "You've got cancer, you're going to die."

The isolation of homeschool created a lifestyle of indoctrination. In my life, we accepted the Bible and religion without question, and our particular Biblical system was all about punishment. For example, I once ate a candy bar I wasn't supposed to. When my mom and stepdad asked me, I lied and denied it. I knew that lying was wrong, but I did it anyway. That incident led to three months of no privileges. I wasn't allowed *anything*: no TV or music. No leaving the house. No friend time, even though I didn't have any to begin with. I wouldn't see the light of day for months.

My grandparents' house was my safe haven during this time; they lived two miles down the road, and I could walk there. When I lost my privileges, I wasn't even allowed to visit them. I had no escape! You won't be surprised to learn that I became depressed and started acting out. I wasn't doing drugs or cussing my parents. But, as any young teenager would, I began to fight back. I began to question, and I found out very quickly that questions would not be tolerated either.

Physical and emotional discipline played a big role at home. After I had been found guilty of something, I had to go outside. There, my stepdad read the Bible to me. There was always a Bible verse that explained why I was such a terrible person. Then, I put both hands on the wall and he administered a spanking with a board he kept for the very purpose of purging my sins. Or at least that is what it appeared to be. He was, he said, "administering religious medicine." Afterwards I was forced to watch Joyce Meyer videos with my stepdad and my mom.

The only videos we watched were the ones that could be twisted to fit their agenda that something was wrong with me. It was the only television they allowed me to watch during my times of imprisonment.

I look back now and see that these were extreme punishments. You, reading this, might be thinking the same thing. At the time, I did not. I didn't think it was unusual to be asked to lean against a wall while my stepfather applied "religious medicine" to me with a board. I thought everyone had the Bible read to them as part of their punishment. I thought it was normal to be grounded for months for eating a Hershey bar. I just didn't *know* any different.

Religion became a real nuisance. *Everything* in my life centered around religion and how I was clearly failing at it. No matter what I did, I could never seem to get anything right. My entire life felt like a boot camp, where you can never get anything right, even when it actually is right (because that's part of the boot camp plan). Boot camp breaks you down, and then very meticulously builds you back up with a specific purpose.

I am still not sure what my parents' purpose was. It wasn't to make me a better person. In the end, the only conclusion I have is that they wanted me to feel one thing: fear. I would ask, "God, why is everything so hectic for me all the time? I never get it right."

Homeschooling under my parents completely isolated me for a year and a half. (Funnily enough, my wife also was homeschooled. When our kids were born, she suggested homeschooling. Does it surprise you that I said, "I'd rather die"?)

I don't believe my parents are, or were, abusive people or parents. Extreme in every sense of the word? Absolutely. Yet it is not lost on me that so many people had it so much worse. Instead, my parents thought they were saving my soul. Still to this day, I believe that about both of them. That is the scary thing about an ideal: right or wrong, people believe it until the end. According to them, I was *the worst person* in the world. No matter what they tried, it was clear that I was going to Hell.

As I said, I actually was a pretty good kid. I never drank a beer until I was eighteen and in the military. I never smoked or even had a girlfriend until my junior year of high school. I was smart, too, getting As and Bs in class. I didn't see that in myself at the time, because all I was told was how bad I was. I was *never* good enough. Now, in my thirties, with three kids of my own, I look back and can see how messed up my home life was. I know now that God is a God of love and mercy, yet when I was a child the Bible was turned against me time and again as a tool to prove how "bad" I was.

At that time, the only God I knew was a bully.

You might assume I'd be against religion forever. Yet I'm a Christian today. I just have a very, very different idea from my stepdad and my mom of what that actually means.

THE OUTCAST YEARS

By the time I got to the middle of seventh grade, my stepdad's and my mother's health had declined so dramatically that she couldn't homeschool me any longer. They enrolled me again into public school, Caledonia Middle School, out of desperation. Personally, I was excited about it. I know that sounds terrible to be excited that your parents were not well, but that's how I felt.

I was thrilled because I didn't know how weird I was and what a learning curve I was about to encounter. You know that stereotypical idea of what a homeschooled kid is like? That weirdo kid nobody understood? Yeah, that was me, 100 percent. When the only people you spend time with are your parents, you get kind of weird. When the only people you spend time with are your parents and they have major physical, mental, and religious issues, you get *really* weird. I didn't realize that eighteen months of isolation would make me so different from everyone else.

I went back to school in January, after the winter holiday. I had never seen so many kids in one place! I was in awe of everyone around me, but I quickly realized how different I was. It took no time at all for me to become an outcast. I couldn't relate to any of the other kids; I didn't know the bands they listened to, the shows they watched, or the sports they played. I didn't have the same clothes. I didn't know which brand of shoes were the cool ones, and therefore lacked approval of just about everyone. I was a good kid, but kids, in general, can be brutal when they don't understand each other. In no time at all, they knew me as "the homeschooled weird kid."

I understand this is nothing too shocking for you to read. I am not saying that I think I was treated unfairly. Nor am I saying it is right to attack anyone for being different. I am just saying that is the world that we live in. Most often, people who are hurting like to hurt other people. Any social worker will tell you that more often than not those who are being unkind to kids at school are most likely treated unkindly at home. It's very simple really. I was an easy target because I was socially awkward and kids did what kids do. It was as simple as that.

Yet, even then, God was working in my life. I would eventually find my footing through a chance meeting. I met this kid by the name of Aaron Brandt. Unlike all the other kids, Aaron didn't judge me so quickly or superficially. I don't remember exactly when we met or when we talked for the first time. Maybe he was at school talking about a sports team and I pretended to be in the know, or maybe it was because we walked the same route to school every morning. Either way, Aaron and I became friends.

Aaron didn't care that I was the homeschooled weird kid. He treated me normally. For the first time ever, I had a friend who I could be a middle-school-aged kid around. We talked about the dumbest things. We talked about all the girls and how "hot" we thought they were, knowing full well neither one of us had any idea what to do if any of those girls were to ever really talk to us. I've often wondered if Aaron knew I was as messed up as I was. Maybe he saw me as a charity case, and because he is a good person, he felt obligated to hang out with me. All I know is that Aaron chose to be my friend at a time in my life when I had no idea who I was, where I was going, or what I was going to do next. Aaron to this day *still* might not realize how much he did to save me. Through his friendship, I started to break out of my awkward shell. He showed me what life was like outside of the prison that was the house on North Wolfe Road. He became my first *real* friend, and twenty years later we are still brothers.

Every morning, my alarm clock went off, I got up, showered, dressed, combed my hair in a stupid combover (somebody really should have told me how dumb I looked), cooked breakfast, and was out the door before my mom and stepdad even were awake. (I didn't think that was strange at the time but looking back on it, I see that was an indicator of my abnormal home life.)

There was Killebrew's hardware store on the corner where Aaron lived. Every single day, he and I would hit that corner together and finish walking to school together.

We also shared one class in seventh grade. Slowly but surely, I began to figure out who I was. Aaron showed me how to move into normality. I don't know what would've happened if I'd never met him.

The more time I spent with Aaron, the more I learned that things at my house weren't exactly all right. He never said anything outright, but I began comparing his household with mine and drawing my own conclusions. I began to think, "Wait a minute—your parents do *what*, or let you do *what*? What's going on at my house? Why don't I get to do any of these things?" As time passed, I began to grow a larger group of friends who helped me see how wrong things were in my home.

The more I learned, the stronger I became—not just physically, but mentally. For once, I began to believe that there wasn't something wrong with me. I began to realize I was just like everyone else. Were we perfect? No one ever is. But we weren't evil!

I stayed in public school as things at home deteriorated. There was more and more turmoil. Even today, my parents probably would

THE MORE I LEARNED, THE STRONGER I BECAME—NOT JUST PHYSICALLY, BUT MENTALLY. FOR ONCE, I BEGAN TO BELIEVE THAT THERE WASN'T SOMETHING WRONG WITH ME. I BEGAN TO REALIZE I WAS JUST LIKE EVERYONE ELSE. WERE WE PERFECT? NO ONE EVER IS. BUT WE WEREN'T EVIL!

tell you that they did what they did to "save my soul," but I know better. They wanted to control me. Every parent does this to some extent, usually out of love, sometimes for darker reasons. Unfortunately, some parents will work out their regrets of what they didn't do or didn't achieve in their own lives on their kids. I was an obsession for mine. I was not only their child, I was their property, and nobody—including me—was going to jeopardize that.

By the time I was a sophomore, my parents were so "ill" and so self-medicated that they repeatedly checked themselves into a mental hospital in Birmingham. They left me alone at home during these times of "self-improvement." Sometimes I wonder what they told other people when they went away. Did no one wonder about the fate of their son, home alone while they were "getting it together"? As far as they were concerned, I was "the crazy one," but I knew even then—and I certainly know now—that wasn't true.

I was frustrated with my life. "God," I thought, "this isn't fair. Why can't I just be who I am? Why do I have to deal with all of this?" It seemed unjust that my parents *certainly* didn't have their lives figured out, yet they were constantly telling me what was wrong with *my* life.

Watching them milk the system, watching them tell themselves that they had some kind of disability and needed all kinds of help, drove me insane. I recognize that people can suffer real problems and need help, but after what I've seen in my own family, I do want to say to them, "prove it." I believe it's too easy to become dependent—dependent on help, and dependent on medicine. You can become so dependent you forget what the real world actually feels like, so that you feel something is wrong with you all the time. When you are constantly medicated, the real world can feel painful. And that's what started to happen to my parents.

Don't get me wrong, my mom lived through more than one true trauma. I am not trying to diminish what happened to her. However, I do think both she and my stepdad forgot what the real world was actually supposed to feel like. The real world isn't always what you want it to be. Living involves more than just the "good" moments. *Real* living includes feeling the joy, sadness, strength, weakness, bliss, and pain. *Real* life is a story, and unfortunately so many people today just want to check out of the journey and only be around for the "highlights."

As I said, I represented failure to my parents. Both my mom and my stepdad felt they had tried everything they could to save me, and nothing was working. By definition, to them anyway, I was *bad*. The fact that I had been saved once at a young age by Jesus didn't matter. The mentality in our household was one of failure. You were either moving forward or you were backsliding, and from their point of view I was always backsliding. Which simply meant I was going to Hell, and apparently by association was dragging them to Hell with me. This was not acceptable!

No matter what I did, I could never win. Until I found a loophole.

CHAPTER 2

EVERY BEGINNING
HAS AN END

In the middle of my sophomore year, I turned to music as a kind of release. I was in the drum line of the band and I started playing guitar.

I actually got to be pretty good, if I may say so myself. Now, I knew there was no chance in the God-loving world that my mom would ever let me be in a rock band, so I chose the next best thing: I went back to the First Assembly of God church. I would play music there.

That was my opportunity. After all, how could my parents complain about my going to church?

By this point, we no longer attended First Assembly of God as a family. My parents considered themselves superior to everyone there. They always found something wrong with the pastor, or the church, or the congregation. They concluded, "We're better Christians than they are." (That was typical of my parents and of a particular kind of "Christian" that rubs me the wrong way, as I will expand upon later in this book.)

So we were "Christians" who never actually went to church?

Fine, I'll just go by myself.

First Assembly of God had become a major church within the city of Columbus, and it included a big youth group called Firestorm: hundreds of kids who met on Wednesday nights. The first time I heard the worship band play, I saw a group of kids my age and knew I could find my purpose among them. In fact, the competitive part of me thought I could be better than them—I could be the lead guy.

I begged to audition, and when the rhythm guitar position opened up, I jumped at the opportunity. I tried out, I got the spot, and soon was playing at church or practicing four or five days a week. We played on Wednesday nights. We traveled to other churches to play for them, and most Sunday nights we played adult service as well. On Sundays, I was at church by 9 am and service was at 10:30 a.m. I had some lunch, went home for four hours, and came back for the next service at 6:30 p.m.

Even though I was out of the house all the time, my parents accepted it because I was at *church*. I was having a good time, but I was very intentional about what I was doing. I had found a way through.

This is how I met my youth pastor, Darrell, who became a father figure to me and hundreds of other kids. (That was a relationship that would later prove, yet again, that people are not always who they appear to be.) I was starting to gain my own understanding of religion through Pastor Darrell. Although he wasn't as extreme as my parents, he was severe in his own way: no backsliding, no secular music, no sitting next to your girlfriend, etc. I didn't mind any of that—after all, I didn't even have a girlfriend. For once, things felt like they were going the right direction. I had a system.

"Man," I thought to myself, "I'm winning on both fronts here."

Little did I realize how Pastor Darrell was going to play a very important—and very, very different—role in my relationship with God in the coming years. It was not at all what I expected. And it was not good.

JUNIOR YEAR

Junior year was both one of the best and worst years of my life.

By junior year, I was a focal figure at the church, spending at least four days a week there. My parents accepted this, and I found a new freedom in it. And soon enough, I found myself falling for a girl named Terri.

This is the first time a particular girl had caught my eye. Picture crazy, hormonal, sixteen-year-old, teenage first love. More accurately think "hormonal nut case!" That's what I felt.

Luckily, she liked me back. We started dating in the first part of the school year. I'd never been happier. For the first time, I felt like I was normal. I waved goodbye to my time as a weird outcast. Not only was I popular, a Christian, and musically talented (the only attribute I had, since I was a skinny kid and certainly no jock); I had a girlfriend to top everything off. I was making something of myself.

But Terri started a spiral with my parents that my family never recovered from. She started a series of traumas for me that I still struggle with to this day. Caroline broke my parents. Terri sent them over the edge completely, and I was about to hit the resulting tidal wave head on. I don't blame her for what happened—quite the opposite, and we remain good friends to this day. Not only do my kids call her Aunt Terri because she married one of my best friends (Will), but she and my wife are best friends! As you'll see, Terri and Aaron are why I finally found the strength to rebel in a way that fundamentally changed my life.

Alongside Terri, I created an entire second family for myself outside of my real family: Will, Aaron, Peter, Charlie, Jeremy, Rusty, Tommy, and Chris Smith. In my junior year, I went from being a social outcast to dating the future homecoming queen and having a great group of people around me.

My mom and stepdad knew that Terri and I were dating, but I was never allowed to do anything with her. As a result, the only time I could see Terri was at church. I would tell my parents I was going to church and drive straight to Terri's house. We *did* actually go to church, but then we'd go hang out, just us. This was our version of a date.

Until we got caught.

My parents didn't walk in on Terri and me. Instead, they got us a different way.

One day, before church, I decided to buy myself a new cell phone. That was a mistake, and when I got home I walked into a trap.

"Where the crap did you get that?" my stepdad asked when he saw the phone. He was always waiting to bust me. He felt that if I was doing something right it was only because I must be hiding something.

"I bought it. I didn't steal it or anything," I said.

"Where'd you buy it?"

"Before church, I stopped off at the Cingular store."

"So you went somewhere other than church?"

Boom. I wasn't allowed to go anyplace besides *church*. Those were the rules. And the Cingular store wasn't *church*.

Busted.

They sentenced me to three months without privileges and took everything: I couldn't go to my grandparent's house; I couldn't go to church; I couldn't see Terri. Remember, I was a teenager in love; I became completely inconsolable. I felt like my parents were taking my life force away from me.

For the first time, I rebelled. In one of their weak moments, I convinced my parents that they couldn't take *church* away from me. I pleaded my own case as hard as I could. (Looking back, I can see that one reason I'm good at what I do today is I learned how to convince my parents of things when I was a teen. I've been pleading my own case for a long time!)

"Okay, fine," I said. "I can't see Terri, fine. I can't go to the movies, fine. I can't watch movies at home, fine. But you can't take church from me. I've got an obligation. I'm supposed to play in the band. You can't let them down."

When my parents finally conceded, I started going behind their back. I went right back to doing what I was doing before. Terri and I were going strong. We were seeing each other all the time. Finally, after three months, I got my privileges back. And for a solid month, things were amazing. Then I got caught again.

Before school, I would pick Terri up at her house. That's a nice, normal thing to do when you are dating someone, but it wasn't something I was *allowed* to do. I never told my parents, because I didn't see the point—I knew what they'd say. So I simply left it out. One day as I was driving to school I saw my stepdad driving toward me in the other lane. As soon as I did, I knew that he'd seen Terri with me in the car.

Busted. Again. I knew my parents would be lying in wait for me when I got home. And they were.

The sentence: I couldn't take Terri to prom, and, of course, I was on house arrest—for six months this time.

I lost my ever-loving mind. How many times could my entire teen-age life be taken away from me? Wouldn't you snap? I didn't go *Carrie* or anything, but this time I didn't just take the punishment lying down. Eventually, we came to a compromise, but what I didn't know was they were planning something much worse. They were planning to get rid of me.

Now, I am aware that this may seem like a small thing looking back, but at the time, it was the last straw. I had had enough. We all had. The following week, what little had been holding us together at home fell apart. My parents decided they couldn't do any more to "save" me. They were going to send me away to French Camp Academy!

THE DAY THAT CHANGED EVERYTHING

French Camp is a religious school for kids who are one step away from jail—real lost causes. The school doesn't advertise itself that way, but that was its reputation. My parents said it was a great school, but any sane person knew what it was and what going there meant. It was a place to get rid of the bad kids you didn't want.

That's how my parents saw me, even though I was a good, church-going kid with good grades. That didn't matter in their worldview. I was a *backslider*. The only thing left to do was take care of the paperwork and then they'd deliver me to the school. I'd be some-one else's problem. That, to me, would be a death sentence. Yes, I would be away from my parents, but I would also be away from my friends, my girlfriend, my church group—my life.

However, in all the madness, my parents did something I never expected. They made a mistake. Or, as I see it, that's when God stepped in on my behalf.

French Camp Academy required three of my teachers to fill out a form of "recommendation" explaining why I would be the ideal candidate for a slot. Rather than take the forms to school themselves, my parents gave them to me in their medicated state and told me to ask the teachers to complete them.

Can you believe the nerve? Take these forms about your own demise and have your teachers fill them out?

I didn't see it then, but that was God watching over me.

They had taken my car away, so like the obedient boy that I was, I walked to school. Aaron offered to drive me, but of course that wasn't allowed either. As I walked that route that Aaron and I had walked a thousand times, I found myself thinking about my entire life. It was as if I was walking in slow motion, and my entire life was flashing before my eyes.

My first class was English, with one of my favorite teachers, Mrs. Richardson. I told her I needed to speak with her after class. When the bell rang, she approached me. I started tearing up. I couldn't hold it back. All I could do was hand her the form and look down in defeat. As she read the form, I could see the disbelief on her face. I could see her thinking, "Is this a joke?"

Everyone was aware my home life was complicated. I expect they had suspicions about my parents. As an adult now, I can see how it would have been difficult not to. Mrs. Richardson looked at me and said something I'll never forget, "Graham, this isn't you. This is ridiculous. What is going on?"

I broke. After years of holding back, I just lost it. I told her everything. Everything that Terry and Aaron had been saying for months wasn't right about my home. Everything that I knew by now was crazy. Mrs. Richardson cried as I cried, and she hugged me. It was a moment when a person who only saw me at school knew more about me than my own parents.

After I was done, she took me to see Mr. Hurt, my chemistry teacher and the assistant band director who coached me in drumline. No one in school knew me better than Mr. Hurt. He looked at the French Camp form and called BS immediately. Both teachers completely broke the teacher façade I was so used to as a student. In that moment, they were no longer Mrs. Richardson and Mr. Hurt. They became Ann and Ben.

"We've got to talk to the principal."

"Heck, no, we're not talking to the principal! Are you guys trying to get me killed?"

They pretty much dragged me to the principal's office, and I told my story for a third time.

"We've got to call Child Services," he said.

"Have you lost your mind, calling Child Services?" I repeated my plea, "Are you trying to get me killed? *I cannot go home ever again if you do this!*"

As an adult, I understand that they had no choice. They had a legal obligation. At the time, I believed that if that conversation didn't fall my way, I was dead, and I didn't want to take that chance.

The situation was urgent; my stepdad was coming to pick me up after lunch to force me to see a counselor, who would do the final sign-off of the forms. I had three hours to figure out a solution, or my life would change forever.

To this day, I find it difficult to understand what happened next. The teachers placed me in the school counselor's room, which had no windows. They shut the door. And I sat there for hours, freaking out. Every now and then someone would open the door to give me an update, "Hey, just letting you know, your parents are here and the social worker is here."

I had no one to talk to. My heart sank, and sank further, into my stomach. I thought I was going to throw up. Strangely, no social worker ever came to talk to me, although standard procedure is that I should have been interviewed. I can only speculate what really happened while I was in that room. To this day, I don't know if the school ever called Child Services or not. All I know is that at 2 o'clock the door opened and there stood my worst nightmare: the principal, my mom, and my stepdad, all looking like they wanted to murder me.

Somehow, this "rescue mission" the principal had set out on had been turned around. In the morning, he had been praising me as a fine young man. In the afternoon, he showed disappointment and utter disgust. My parents had convinced everyone that I was a sick, crazy, liar. I don't know if the principal actually believed it and his hands were tied, or if he didn't believe it at all. Whatever the truth in his heart, I know this: he caved. He caved in to their pressure.

In the end, my worst nightmare happened. I was to be sent home with my parents. I knew my world was coming to an end. But God was working. I just didn't know it. Even in our darkest times, God is with us. He is always working in our lives, even when it seems like all is lost.

On the car ride to what I was certain was my utter demise, nobody said a word. Mom sat in the front of the red Jeep Grand Cherokee while my stepdad drove. Nobody cried. Nobody screamed. Nobody asked, "how could you do this to us?!" Nobody spoke a word! It was silent! They didn't act like two parents who were hurt and devastated by the actions of a misguided teen. They had the demeanor of two people who couldn't believe I had the balls to *out* them the way that I had.

Simply put, I knew that my life was over. However, at the flashing traffic light, something purely miraculous happened. To this day, I know that this moment in my life was truly in God's hands. You see, we should have turned right toward our house, but we didn't. As I sat in the back of the car with my head hung in defeat, I felt the car go left.

"They are taking me to French Camp right now," I thought. I would never be seen or heard from again. This is the end of every horror movie ever, where they try to get rid of the body.

Instead, they pulled up in front of my grandparents' house.

IN THE END, MY WORST NIGHTMARE HAPPENED. I WAS TO BE SENT HOME WITH MY PARENTS. I KNEW MY WORLD WAS COMING TO AN END. BUT GOD WAS WORKING. I JUST DIDN'T KNOW IT. EVEN IN OUR DARKEST TIMES, GOD IS WITH US. HE IS ALWAYS WORKING IN OUR LIVES, EVEN WHEN IT SEEMS LIKE ALL IS LOST.

"Get out," my stepdad said. "Go inside and stay inside. Your grandparents are at our house."

By the grace of God, instead of experiencing the life-ending punishment I expected at his hands, I was standing in the driveway as he and my mom drove away to a conference with Maw and Paw about my fate.

I had no idea what was going on. I didn't know what to do. I felt deeply betrayed by the adults I finally had trusted. I couldn't think clearly. Terri and Aaron were still in school, so I couldn't reach them, and they had no idea what was happening. Instead, I called Terri's older brother and told him what had happened and to please relay the message. He couldn't really do anything to help me at the time, so I felt betrayed by him, too. I trusted him, and I expected him to take me out of there. Now as an adult, I realize that people can't just go and literally kidnap someone's kid. However, at the time I felt betrayed by everyone.

In all the madness, I wish I'd called my dad that day. That would have been the obvious thing to do, but my head was all over the place. He lived almost six hours away, in Spanish Fort, Alabama. Since my mom remarried, our relationship slowly had begun to heal. We talked occasionally on the phone, and I visited him on holidays. It wasn't the relationship we have now, but it was something. For some reason, I didn't even think about calling him.

I had nothing else to do, so I sat on my grandparents' couch and watched TV. Hours went by. I thought to myself, "what could possibly be taking so long?" At this point, I wanted whatever was going to happen to just happen. I couldn't take the silence. If my life was going to be over, let's get it over with already.

Then the phone rang.

My grandparents had (at the time) state-of-the-art technology: caller ID that displayed on the television. That's when I saw the name. It was a familiar name. It was a name I had known all my life.

My dad was calling.

I answered the phone and heard my dad's voice, "Hey man, what's up?" he asked.

"Not much," I said.

Not much?! My whole world was falling apart, and all I could say was "not much?!" What was I, some kind of idiot?!

There was a pause. "Are you sure?"

I was so stupid I didn't realize that he already knew what was going on. In fact, he knew everything.

God was taking a hand in my fate. You see, my mother, believing that my soul was a lost cause to her, had come up with a plan to send me away. I was a problem, and the problem would be made to disappear. However, she didn't call my dad, because she and my dad hated each other. But she did call my dad's sister, Aunt Lilly.

Mom and Aunt Lilly were not on speaking terms by any means, but my aunt knew things were not good at my house. If you step back and look at it, my mom called someone who was basically a stranger to her out of the blue and asked her to take her kid off her hands—and believe it or not, my Aunt Lilly said yes.

She agreed to make the seven-hour drive from Florida and take me in. For this to work, though, she would have to convince my parents to sign custody over to her.

AUNT LILLY INTERVENES

My mom and Aunt Lilly hated each other. Yet in the end, Aunt Lilly, Granny, my mom, my stepdad, Maw, and I all sat together in my parents' house while my mother went on and on about all the terrible things I had done, and all the ways I was a lost cause.

Aunt Lilly and Granny—my dad's mom, who lived with my aunt— kept agreeing. It was hard to listen to.

"You're right," Aunt Lilly said to my parents. "You've done every-thing you can. There comes a point where you have to wash your hands of him. We'll take him out of this atmosphere and he'll either turn it around or he won't, but you've done all you can do. You can't help how he's turned out."

It was devastating to hear. Was I really such a horrible person? Did I actually deserve this? Even though I felt like I was dying inside, I kept my mouth shut and watched my mother sign the legal documents that gave me to my Aunt Lilly. (Actually, she only signed power of attorney papers; Aunt Lilly was just trying to get me out of the house, and these were the fastest documents she could execute. Her goal was to get me out and in front of an attorney who could help me. It turned out that since I was sixteen, I was legally able to choose where I lived. I just didn't know that then.)

When it came time to leave, my mom got up to hug me and tell me how much she actually loved me. I thought, "What are you doing? I just watched you sign me away in the living room!"

We loaded up the car and I said my goodbyes to Maw. That was utterly crippling to me. Maw knew her daughter was insane. Yet, she was powerless to stop what was happening. I might as well have been her son, and she was losing me.

The last real exchange I had with my stepdad were the last words anyone from my Caledonia family would say to me that night. As I was leaving, he leaned in, shook my hand and said, "I know you're going to Hell, and we tried everything to save you. Good riddance."

I will never forget those words. I will never forget the look in his eyes. I will never forget how terrified I was. *"I know you are going to Hell."* To this day, everything I do has an attachment to that moment and to those words. I knew he was wrong, and I would spend the rest of my life proving him wrong.

That was the last thing he ever said to me.

When we got in the car, Aunt Lilly dropped the mask. She turned to me and said, "Don't worry baby, you are safe now. You're never going back there again. We love you, and we believe you!"

Granny looked across the front seat at her and said, "That woman is batshit crazy!"

I don't think Aunt Lilly will ever know how much she changed my life in that moment. I can go down the rabbit hole over and over again about what my life might have been like at French Camp Academy or, worse, if I had stayed with my mother...but who really knows?

In the end, it was my aunt, my dad, and my grandparents who saved me. It was my family three states away who listened to what God was telling them to do. As far as my aunt's family goes, they had no obligation to me. I was just a nephew. Yet they chose to love me as their own in that moment.

They showed me what grace and love actually mean. They *chose* me!

Sometimes, *choosing* someone means more than "I love you" ever will.

I know now that God was with me every step of the way.

When I look back, it doesn't make any sense that things happened the way they did. It doesn't make sense for my mother to sign away her child. The only way it makes sense is if I see that God was working to put me on the path he intended for me to go down.

Lilly and my grandmother told me to not pay attention to a word they had said in the living room. All the agreeing they had done, all the terrible things they had said, had been an act to make sure my mother didn't change her mind at the last minute.

They were deeply compassionate. Instead of leaving that day, they'd made arrangements to stay another night at my Aunt Kathy's house, nearby, so I could say goodbye to Terri. We also made one last stop at the school to get all the transfer documents I would need to start school in Florida.

I saw Mr. Hurt, who said, "Go in peace." A simple statement, but one I cherished in a moment that felt like the end of something.

And then we left. The next day I was in Gulf Breeze, Florida. It felt like a different continent to me in 2003. We were right on the beach; nobody drove trucks; and everyone seemed different. Nice, but definitely different. My aunt enrolled me in the local high school so I could finish the last three months of my junior year.

I couldn't believe what my life had become. Although I felt depressed and miserable, there was nothing I could do. My father wanted me to move to Alabama for my senior year, but the truth was all I wanted to do was get back to Caledonia. That's where my life was.

The reason my dad and I have a good relationship today is because he understood that, to do right by me, he needed to facilitate my move back to Mississippi. Before the start of senior year, my mom's parents (Maw and Paw)—the people I felt, and still feel, are my real parents, and who gave me my real moral education—agreed to take me in.

And that's what happened. My dad decided to be the best dad he could for me in that moment. He knew deep down he couldn't make up for the past. It was what it was. He knew I needed him to be something else at this point in my life. So he didn't fight it.

Just like that, I was back where I belonged: in Mississippi, and as haunting as my past may have been, I was home.

CHAPTER 3

NOT YOUR AVERAGE WAR STORY

By the start of senior year, I was back home in Caledonia, Mississippi. Life was good. I had almost completely cut ties with my parents who, weirdly, tried to get custody of me again. I had turned seventeen by then and spoken to a lawyer. I knew I had the legal right to decide where I lived.

I think they wanted me back because they wanted control. In the grand scheme of things, I had won! I had gotten away from them and was living the life I wanted to live, the one they thought was ensuring my trip to Hell. I was in the very situation that had made them so mad to begin with, and I was in charge. They tried to threaten me to get me back, but I knew my rights. I wasn't going back. I was *never* going back. Now, at thirty-three years old, I still haven't gone back.

I was back with Terri. We were so ridiculous in our teenage love that we arranged to have every class together. In October, she became homecoming queen. I was dating the homecoming queen in my senior year! I'd come a long way from my time as the weird homeschooled kid. I remember thinking, "This is it. This is gonna be my life. We will get married, have kids, and grow old together."

During our school's homecoming celebration, Terri's brother, Jesse, walked her onto the field. I was on the field with the drumline playing the music for her. I still remember looking at her and thinking, *how did I get so lucky*? Jesse was a veteran of the Iraq war who had deployed during the initial invasion, back in Caledonia as a recruiter. I didn't know it then, but Jesse was going to change my life in a very different way than Terri was about to.

Despite what I thought, Terri wasn't the one who God had planned for me. Despite what I thought, I wasn't perfect for her either. That's something else I would have to learn in my life. Other people have lives too and have just as much right to live them the way that they want to live them. Homecoming night was a high point that almost immediately became the lowest point. Toward the end of that evening, I thought we would celebrate. However, when I finally saw and got to speak to Terri, I knew something had changed. She told me she was going to a friend's house for a sleepover. Why is this weird? Terri and I spent every minute together. This definitely was weird.

You ever have one of those moments where you know what's going to happen but you still just let it play out, hoping you are wrong? That was exactly what this felt like. By the time the weekend was over, she had dumped me.

I was devastated.

Now that we are adults, I often wonder if she stayed with me as long as she did out of a feeling of obligation. After all, my life was *messed up*! No moral person could dump me while I was going through the Hell I did. If that was the case, she was a saint to tolerate me until she knew I was finally in a safe place. At the time, it hurt me more than I knew how to process.

Terri symbolized everything I had been fighting for: acceptance, popularity, young love, freedom. Suddenly, she was gone. It was beyond painful, and I played it like I was in a bad rom-com: crying in bed for the first twenty-four hours, missing school, eating chocolate, and wanting never to step foot into the outside world again.

Thank God for Aaron! After about a week, he came over to my house, took one look at me, and said, "I don't know what this is, but you're going to have to snap out of it!"

Today, I'm so embarrassed by that behavior that if I could travel back in time, I'd slap myself. I was in high school, and high school was my whole life. Much like teenagers today dealing with their own issues, I didn't realize, nor could I understand, that high school is just a blip on the radar. I had so much life left to live. It was all going to be okay. For now, however, the hits would keep coming.

One month after our breakup, I learned that Terri was *engaged* to an Army ROTC cadet named John Hawkins who was attending Mississippi State. How could a seventeen-year-old senior in high school compete with that? I could barely afford to take Terri to Taco Bell once a week, and this guy was in the Army?!

I was screwed.

TERRI SYMBOLIZED EVERYTHING I HAD BEEN FIGHTING FOR: ACCEPTANCE, POPULARITY, YOUNG LOVE, FREEDOM. SUDDENLY, SHE WAS GONE. IT WAS BEYOND PAINFUL, AND I PLAYED IT LIKE I WAS IN A BAD ROM-COM: CRYING IN BED FOR THE FIRST TWENTY-FOUR HOURS, MISSING SCHOOL, EATING CHOCOLATE, AND WANTING NEVER TO STEP FOOT INTO THE OUTSIDE WORLD AGAIN.

A FRITO WRAP AND SONIC CHANGED MY LIFE

If you look at me now, you wouldn't believe that I was a scrawny kid. Trust me, I was. I was 5'10" or 5'9", depending on the time of day, and weighed 130 pounds in my senior year of high school. Back then, I respected the military, as just about everybody in Mississippi does, but I never thought it was the place for me. I was a scrawny musician, not a military guy. Still, I was exposed a lot to the military, because Caledonia was a suburb of Columbus, which is home to Columbus Air Force Base. Although I never saw the military as part of my future, I respected the men and women who joined, but I never saw myself wearing a uniform.

Like most people, I vividly remember the 9/11 attacks, which happened while I was a freshman in high school. A lot of our teachers were reservists who went away to war in the months following that attack. I didn't know then that eventually I would follow.

Aaron, on the other hand, had wanted to join the military his whole life. During senior year, he wanted to go to the recruiting office in Columbus, but when push came to shove, he was too nervous to go alone. He was so nervous he was afraid even to ask me to go with him. But he was excited, too. I agreed to go along if he bought me a Frito chili pie at Sonic in return. Like any hormonal teenager, I was constantly hungry and very food motivated. He might be signing up to serve his country, but I had something more important on my mind: a Frito Chili Cheese Wrap.

Terri's brother Jesse was a recruiter at the Army National Guard office, so that's who Aaron wanted to talk to. I sat and minded my own business while Aaron talked to Jesse about the Army. Not surprisingly, I quickly attracted the attention of another recruiter, Sergeant First Class Hawk.

"Hey, bud," he said. "Let me ask you something. You ever been in trouble with the law?"

"No, sir."

"You smoke any of that stuff?"

"No."

Then, he took out a piece of paper and wrote down a math problem: $(2X+4)(2X-4)$. I solved it and he said, "Yes, you'll do!"

I am not sure what happened next. I really don't know how Sergeant Hawk got inside my head, but he did. What made me sign up for the Army National Guard for a six-year tour? Maybe I wanted to prove something to Terri, who had decided she preferred an ROTC cadet to me. Maybe I was attracted by the idea of going to war and doing something for my country. Maybe I was a dumb seventeen-year-old who didn't know any better.

Before I knew it, I was in Jackson, Mississippi enlisting into the US Army. I turned eighteen on January 29 and enlisted on February 2 as part of the Army National Guard.

At the time, there was a big stigma in Mississippi surrounding the Guard. They were seen as a bunch of good old boys who got together one weekend a month and drank a lot of beer. This was before the Iraq deployments, when Guard troops were sent to war for longer than regular Army troops. I joined the Guard because I wasn't sure I was ready for active duty Army and, to tell the truth, because I wasn't sure I could make it there.

After I enlisted, I had to attend monthly Recruitment Sustainment Program (RSP) drills through the rest of my senior year to learn about rank structure and other military standards. These took place in Starkville, home to Mississippi State. These drills were taught by NCOs and cadets, including John Hawkins—the cadet who took my girlfriend away. I told you this part of my life played out like an American Pie movie. At this point, it was just ridiculous!

However, I must say this: Terri and John didn't work out either. As fate would have it, John would go on to become one of my closest friends/brothers. However, fate would play a hand no one would have anticipated and John was taken from us in a tragic car crash right before he was supposed to be in Ellisa's and my wedding. In his honor, my oldest son is named Johnathon Gage Allen.

He truly was a one-of-a-kind type of guy, and we all miss him to this day.

As the spring season progressed, I worried that I would not make it through boot camp. As I said, I weighed 130 pounds. I had never undertaken a physical challenge in my life. I had never run a mile or lifted a weight bar. But I was actually enjoying the RSP work, and when I look back I realize this was the moment when I began to be shaped into the man I am today. Plus, I learned that I could get promoted to E2 (which meant earning more money) if I could convince anyone to enlist, so I got busy. We were on it! By the time it was all said and done about half my friends and 30 percent of the senior class had enlisted in some military branch. In the end, Aaron, Tommy, Chris Smith, Ty Schneider, Chad Scranton, and I were all part of the Army National Guard.

BOOT CAMP

I am a big believer in the idea that everything happens for a reason, even if the reason isn't immediately clear. I graduated high school on May 19, 2005 and left for boot camp on May 28. That day, Aaron, Chris, and I were supposed to get on a bus to Jackson and then fly out to Fort Jackson, South Carolina. We showed up with about twenty people from different schools to ship out together. But something was wrong with Chris's paperwork, so he had to be held back and couldn't get on the bus with us.

"You'll catch up to your friends at reception," a sergeant told him.

I never saw Chris again.

Reporting to boot camp was as fun as it sounds. Everyone was yelling and throwing stuff around—they were trying to disorient us with planned chaos. Aaron and I had been told that we could take advantage of "the buddy system" and go through boot camp together. We were looking forward to that. As soon as we got off the bus, we were instructed to stand behind one of four buckets. I lined up behind one bucket and he stood right next to me, behind another. What they hadn't told us was those buckets represented different platoons. We'd actually chosen two different platoons! So we ended up in boot camp together all right, and we'd pass each other every day, but we literally could not talk to each other. Talk about a military sense of humor.

While we were in boot camp, I got a letter from a girl I knew back home (letters were the only communication we had). I opened it and began to read: "Graham, I don't know how to start this letter, so I guess I will get right to the point. Chris passed away in a car accident. His funeral is in three days." I was reading a week-old letter about Chris's death and funeral, which had taken place the week before! Up until that moment, Aaron and I expected him to show up at Fort Jackson at any moment!

The truth is simply this: life is fragile. Life is not always kind, and none of us actually deserve anything. Life is precious, and it can be taken away in a moment. So ask yourself: Did you live today like it was your last? I know that's a cliché, but it's the truth. None of us know when it's over, so we'd better live like we cherish life.

Because his paperwork wasn't in order, Chris had to wait to ship out. A few days after Aaron and I left Caledonia, while he waited for his paperwork to be sorted out, he went to a party. He hadn't been drinking, but he got a ride with someone who had. The truck went off the road; Chris was thrown from it and killed. Something as simple as a messed-up form led to his death.

The one time during boot camp that I got to talk to Aaron was when my sergeant gave me sixty seconds to run to his platoon and share the news. "Chris is dead," is all I had time to say. Honestly, it's all I could think to say. What else was I supposed to say? Then I had to run back.

Chris was supposed to be with us. One wrong piece of paperwork sent him down a totally different path. If Aaron and I weren't at boot camp, we definitely would've been at that party too. All three of us could've shared the same fate. Even while writing this, I realize how small life really is. It is over when it's over, so make your mark while you can.

Why do bad things happen to good people? It's a question we are not meant to answer. The Lord is very clear that we are not able to see the magnitude of His plan. We cannot see the path as we walk upon it, but when we turn around, we can see what led us here. Obviously, a piece of paper didn't kill Chris, but it started a chain reaction. It's crazy that I ended up in the military because I was always hungry and would go to a recruiting station in exchange for food. That craving for Sonic put me on the path I am on today and led to everything I am and I have—my military career, my fateful first video, my Daily Rants, my wife, my family, and more. Life is simply strange that way.

I wish I could've said goodbye to Chris, but life isn't as fair as that. I have lost three of my best friends in life, ironically all in cars. Every year, I make an effort to act as though I'm doing something that they'd be proud of. I lost two friends in the month of April so, every April, I drink three beers for the three of them.

THE OTHER 99 PERCENT

People who aren't in the military hear about Special Forces and Navy SEALs and sniper units, and they might imagine that those are typical experiences. Those of us who make up the vast majority of the regular military—the other 99 percent—have experiences a lot more like mine. We all have our own stories. This one is mine.

After I got off the bus that first day at Fort Jackson, South Carolina, I thought, "Well, you made it out. Now what?" From my very first day at boot camp, as part of Second Platoon E 1/34, I had it in my head that I wouldn't make it through. Let me be *very* clear; I was *nothing* special and never wanted to be. I was just a guy looking to go away and say I did my part. Honestly, I am very proud of that.

I still weighed 130 pounds when I showed up. But somewhere in the six months of boot camp and Advanced Individual Training (AIT), the military went from being something I was unsure about to something I was actually pretty good at. I guess I did have something to thank my mom and stepdad for. I never got in trouble; my drill sergeants loved me. (Well, they didn't want to murder me like others, so I consider that to be love.) Being in the military brought out something in me which I'd never discovered before. It brought out a part of me that believed in myself!

Nowadays, boot camps are easier than they used to be because there are different rules than in the old days. Everyone talks about how their boot camp was the hardest and how other boot camps have it easy. The truth is, it all depended on who your drill sergeants were. In my experience, boot camp was not *that* hard. The rules didn't bother me—after all, for years I'd lived in a house and gone to a church with very strict rules. "If I don't know who you are at the end of this cycle," the drill sergeant told us, "you did it right."

I was the exact guy that sergeant wanted me to be. I didn't speak that much. Everyone knew me, but no one would really recognize me. I never got into any individual trouble. I just did my thing.

After boot camp in Fort Jackson, I was transferred to Fort Gordon for additional schooling, called Advance Individual Training, where I learned my actual job: communication specialist for a combat engineer unit. A combat unit is made up of various groups of people: combat specialists, support specialists, medics, truck drivers, cooks, and so on. A communications specialist could be attached to almost any unit—I was attached to a unit of combat engineers. They did the opposite of what you think engineers do. They didn't build houses and bridges; they blew things up.

I finished AIT in December of 2006, and I felt pretty good. I had put on thirty-five pounds, too—Because I was in the Guard, I was expected to go back home, have a life, and train one weekend a month. I realized that the part of this experience that I loved was over. I wasn't working full time any longer in the Army, and I didn't like that one bit.

I got back to Mississippi just before Christmas and enrolled in a few community college classes, which I hated. I was offered drum scholarships to go to other colleges, but I turned them down. As much a part of my life that had been, it was an old chapter that I didn't want to open again. I stuck it out at school for four months, but it just was not me.

My opportunity came in April, at the final formation drill of our Guard unit. By that point I basically hated my life. The Guard, meanwhile, had undergone a transformation. Our unit now contained veterans who had spent eighteen months in Iraq. Those guys had earned their stripes as warriors. That was what I wanted.

At final formation, the first sergeant announced that a unit needed volunteers for Iraq. He asked if anybody wanted to go, and everyone laughed. Everyone except me. I had my arm up.

"I'll do it, Top," I said. "Get me the crap out of here!"

Now, why did I do that? I couldn't really tell you. Maybe I thought that would make me feel I'd really played my role the way I was supposed to. Maybe I thought girls would like me more if I had seen combat. All I knew was, I'm going!

I found myself attached to a transportation unit that was to run daily missions with Heavy Equipment Transports (HETs) in Iraq. The HET team was responsible for pulling logistical supplies from FOB (forward operating base) to FOB in Iraq. They drove big trucks, transporting large items like Abrams tanks. I was the commo guy attached to two units which really had nothing to do with the job I had trained for. But President Bush had just approved the surge back into Iraq, and units were being stood up left and right to get back into combat.

I ended up going AGR (Active Guard Reserve) and spent twelve years in the Army. Ninety percent of National Guard members sign up for one weekend a month and two weeks a year of training. I was part of the other 10 percent that went full time. I wanted to be deployed. When I look back on my twelve years in the Army, I really only think about my first two deployments to Iraq. Those were the times I felt I was doing something of real value. That was when I met four guys who would become my closest friends—guys I would die for, and who would die for me. I learned what family actually looked like, for the first time. And it was during those deployments that I met, dated, and proposed to a woman I am not worthy of to this day.

OFF TO IRAQ

Our unit was scraped together with volunteers from different Guard units. Though I didn't know this at the time, I met people who would shape the next part of my life: Eric Fry, Tom Shepard, Jeff Fargo, and Patrick Chausse, who we called Chassis. This was everyone on my first deployment except for Eric. He was the grandpa of the group at thirty-five, when we were all eighteen. He was so old he had already been in Desert Storm as a Corpsman for the Navy. (I'm sure he will enjoy reading that part.)

AT FINAL FORMATION, THE FIRST SERGEANT ANNOUNCED THAT A UNIT NEEDED VOLUNTEERS FOR IRAQ. HE ASKED IF ANYBODY WANTED TO GO, AND EVERYONE LAUGHED. EVERYONE EXCEPT ME. I HAD MY ARM UP.

"I'LL DO IT, TOP," I SAID. "GET ME THE CRAP OUT OF HERE!"

We soon became as close as brothers. We were the most redneck group you could imagine. Eric was the senior medic. We had a couple of truck drivers, several combat engineers, some reclassified infantry, and a couple of military police to remind us that we didn't suck *that* badly—they got that title. I filled the role of the acting signal NCO.

Tom, Jeff, and Chassis were all infantry guys who had volunteered to form part of the unit. We were surrounded by a lot of active duty people: combat engineers, cooks, truck drivers, infantry guys.

In June we went to Camp Shelby, Mississippi, a huge training base, for mobilization, which means training and getting equipment together. Four months later, in October 2006, we got on a plane headed to Kuwait.

If you picture a stereotypical desert, you're picturing exactly what Kuwait looks like. There's practically nothing else there. Luckily, it was October, so it wasn't as hot as it could've been, but we did have to become acclimated to the weather. Once we got there, we had an acclimation period of around ten days. We were put into *huge* tents. Each tent was the size of a building and had hundreds of cots inside. The lights were on for only about three hours a day. The time shift messed everybody up, so people slept at all hours.

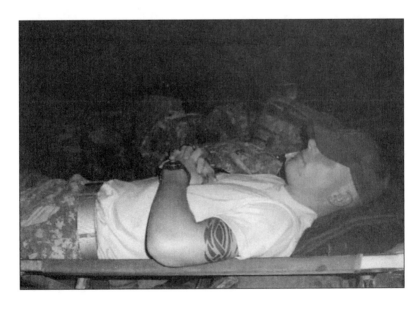

After ten days in Kuwait, we loaded into a C130 that would take us to Iraq. Everyone huddled inside on netting. As we were coming in to land, I heard a strange noise and asked one of the Air Force guys on the plane what it was. "Don't worry about it, it's fine," he said.

Turned out we'd taken some small arms fire, which damaged a window, and one of the engines had stopped working. We didn't know any of this until after we landed, and I appreciate that. I would have flipped out and not been able to do anything about it in the air. However, it introduced me very quickly to how different Iraq was. People just behaved differently. Anyone who has ever been will tell you the same thing. There is just something about it that's terrible, but you can never really leave, either.

CAMP TAJI

I was in Iraq for just over twelve months for my first deployment. I was at Camp Taji for the first seven months, under Fourth Infantry Division (ID). After that, First ID at Camp Liberty needed some help, so a small group of us from Taji were moved to Camp Liberty for the remainder of our time.

Camp Taji was right off Route Tampa, the main north-south route in Iraq. Taji was divided into the US side and Iraqi side and had two main entrances. Our entrance was Gunners Gate, which was on the Iraqi side. It was called the Iraqi side, because the Iraqi Army was still working with us on that side of the base.

The US side had nice two-man rooms in the barracks. On the Iraqi side—which we called the ghetto side—we occupied one of Saddam's special forces barracks. Our room was about twenty feet on a side and slept ten of us. I had a wall locker and a poncho that I hung up, and I used the back of somebody else's wall locker to section off some space for myself. That was all the space I had, a bed and a wall locker. My bed was a door propped up by MRE boxes. For over twelve months, I slept on a door and a mattress about three inches thick. Welcome to Iraq.

That tiny room is where all of our bonding took place. That's also where we would mess with people. For example, whenever somebody yelled "Headphones!" you had to put your headphones on, otherwise you'd risk hearing someone taking care of himself.

Hey, this was Iraq, okay? Don't get all PC on me now. *Trust me,* I will spare you all of the truly disgusting things. However, since I was living in a room full of dudes for over a year, what did you expect? Nobody stopped doing what they were doing, we just put headphones on without missing a beat. A short while later, they'd yell "All clear!" At that point you knew it was safe to not only come out of your area, but also to remove the headphones and not risk hearing noises you can *never* unhear. Most people would find that disgusting or even perverse, but the command "Headphones!" became perfectly normal.

My first deployment was very different from the second. The first deployment took place during the surge, which meant a lot of equipment, a lot of people, and a lot of playing catch-up. It was President Bush's attempt to overtake Iraq with an abundance of military force. Usually, the MP unit was in charge of security and the transportation unit was actually transporting equipment. During the surge, everybody was helping with everything.

We didn't have the sort of armor in place on vehicles that troops have now. Armor was being retrofitted onto vehicles to defend against IED attacks. When the Frag 5 armored door kits came in, E3s like me helped get the armor on. After a mission, while NCOs would backbrief the commanders on the previous mission, five of us peasants would push big metal doors up to a Humvee while the mechanics bolted it in.

There was a lot of fighting outside the wire during daylight hours, and the HETs were too big to maneuver out of fights if we were attacked. As a result, it was safer for us to carry out our operations at night, so that's when we went out. Once we went, we could be gone for days or even weeks at a time.

When we first arrived in theater, we were expected to do RSRs (Right Seat Rides) with the outgoing unit so we could get a feel for how things operated and the lay of the land. We rode with people who showed us what to do and how to do it. The first time out the gate, I was driving one of the HETs on a night mission—picture a huge eighteen-wheeler headed out into the dark.

Before you go out on a mission, you always do a number of pre-combat checks and inspections, and one of the things leadership does is specify what you have to wear. We were at the wire, about to go out the gate, when somebody asked me, "Where's your eye pro?" Well, I didn't have any eye protection with me. I was supposed to, but I didn't. I had to have eye pro—those were the rules. We weren't going out without it.

There was a whole line of trucks behind me. I couldn't back up if I wanted to. I rummaged around and found my sunglasses. "Put 'em on," someone said.

Did you catch that? My very first combat mission outside of the wire in Iraq I was driving around like an idiot with sunglasses on *at night*! I drove out into the Iraqi night for the first time feeling entirely blind. "I am going to die right here," I thought. "I couldn't see a bomb if there was one. I can't see what I'm doing." About the only thing I could see was the taillights of the vehicle ahead of me, and that's what kept me on the road.

Sometimes we were out of Taji for two weeks straight on a mission. We'd haul tanks, Abrams, and M1s, to different FOBs. Once we hauled a canoe and tampons. Yep, you heard me! "Imagine dying over tampons," Eric said. When daylight came, we slept in trucks at whatever base we happened to be in. The next night, we loaded up and headed out again, moving other equipment somewhere else. We went everywhere, from Stryker to Fallujah to Cross Sabers to Hammer to Anaconda to War Horse.

In places like War Horse, a mortar attack was a much bigger deal than it was at Taji. Taji was a big base. Although we were mortared there all the time, the odds of them hitting us were small. Our very first mortar attack though, seemed like a big deal at the time. When the alarm sounded, we had to get into defensive positions, and Chausse and I were tasked with going up to the roof and taking up defensive positions, defending Gunners Gate. I looked back at Chausse, knowing we were being mortared and realizing we were fully exposed on the roof, and thought, *how does it make any sense for us to be up here? Whose idea was this?*

The closest we came to a significant mortaring was when a round hit the motor pool but didn't detonate. A bunch of us sat in lawn chairs and hung out as the Explosives Ordinance Disposal (EOD) team came to blow the mortar up.

In the end, I completed more than 200 missions between both deployments outside the wire. I consider myself blessed to have had the experience I did. On one trip an RPG flew right between our trucks. Another time, a Humvee went over a median right in front of us. We followed and the truck behind us got hit by an IED. No one was hurt, but that tire will never be the same! Another time we were driving during the initial surge down Route Tampa and saw a couple of body bags on the side of the road.

We did have a situation that got a little crazy. The back trailer of a HET had been hit by an IED. We all got out and scanned the vehicle to assess the damage. A guy named Boone hopped out to look at the trailer. The second he bent over to look underneath, the hydraulics exploded right in his face. Someone called a medevac helicopter, and I was chosen to fly with Boone to a nearby base called Cross Sabers. By chosen I mean in about five seconds I was volun-told (told I would be "volunteering") that I would be on the helicopter with Boone. I jumped in with him and was gone.

But then I was stuck. Boone was evacuated back to the States, but I had trouble finding a ride back to Taji. Despite popular belief, everything in the Army isn't always "figured out." What I didn't know was that while I was chilling out at Cross Sabers, my family thought I was MIA. One of the guys in my unit, Eric, had spoken to his wife and said, "Yeah, Graham's gone, we don't know where he is." That simple message spiraled through the grapevine at home to the point where my parents thought I was missing in action. You could always count on Eric to say something that would either be amazing or the dumbest statement ever. This particular time, it was the latter.

Seven days later, when I finally got back to Taji, I called my dad. He and my stepmother were falling all over themselves with relief. They had spent all that time thinking I was dead or missing. "What are you talking about?" I said. "I was just at the hospital with Boone."

That was pretty typical for the way things went for me in Iraq.

On another mission, I did something that in retrospect was phenomenally stupid, but at the time seemed perfectly ordinary, even funny.

We had a lot of cases of people getting burned from IED blasts and fires in vehicles. This was before flame-resistant uniforms were distributed to us, so we rode around in tanker uniforms, which were flame resistant. They were also hot as balls. One night we were out on a mission and I was riding in the back of the HET cab. It was so hot in that thing. I did what every soldier has done (even if they don't admit to it) and took my helmet and IBA (Individual Body Armor) off. I had my uniform unzipped and tied around my waist and my Alabama hat on. (For the whole time I was in Iraq, I carried my Alabama hat with me. In fact, I took that exact hat with me on every single mission. It currently resides at my dad's house, and still has some Iraq sand on it.) I was rednecking everything. If I was going to get blown up, I wanted to be comfortable when it happened.

That night the driver raked the side of the trailer against something, trashing the back of the vehicle. The call came out on the radio for someone to hop out and assess how to move it. I was just sitting there, so I volunteered. I grabbed my weapon and jumped out of the vehicle's cab. The other guys in the convoy couldn't believe what they were seeing. Nobody walked around Iraq without body armor and helmet on, and here I was, under the headlights, strolling around in a T-shirt and my Alabama hat, having a look-see at the trailer. I was a sitting duck.

"Is that effing Allen out there with nothing on?" somebody asked over the radio.

I was in the middle of a war zone in Iraq with absolutely no protection. The scariest part is that it didn't even occur to me that anything was wrong. I had become so desensitized to the risk of war. I was this dumb Mississippi kid just living his life, walking around like a moron.

I definitely got in trouble for that little stunt. The higher-ups were going to charge me under Article 15 of the Military Code of Conduct, which is one of the worst types of administrative punishment you can get. This would be meaningful disciplinary action against my record. I could have been busted down in rank and lost my pay.

Because we were at the height of the surge and everybody was needed, they didn't do that. Instead, I stood at attention in front of the sergeant major and commander while Lieutenant Wells cussed me out. When he was done, the commander said, "I'm leaving the lieutenant to decide what to do with you." He and the sergeant major walked out.

Lieutenant Wells looked at me. "That is the dumbest thing I've ever seen," he said, "but my gosh if that is not the funniest thing I've ever heard in my life."

In the end, I didn't get the worst punishment that I could have, and that I deserved. I was banished to a week of work in the DFAC (Dining Facility). For twelve hours every night I sat in front of the DFAC and checked everybody's ID. It was as ridiculously boring as it sounds. However, I did get to have what I like to call Private First Class justice.

One day a major came to the DFAC without his CAC Card. You see, I wasn't supposed to let anyone in without a CAC Card, not even a major.

"Are you really not gonna let me in?" he demanded.

"Sir," I replied, "for all I know you are a silent shopper trying to find out if I'm doing my job or not, and I'm not getting into trouble again."

In that rare moment I, a Private First Class, got to watch a major take the walk of shame back to his area. It was a moment that probably was more fun than it should have been, but I feel the lower enlisted military members will understand.

I left the United States when I was nineteen and turned twenty in Iraq. My unit returned to the states in October of 2007, four months before my twenty-first birthday. I had been to war and made it back, yet I still couldn't buy a drink. Talk about getting thunder kicked in the face!

While we demobilized at Camp Shelby, an opportunity came up

for Guardsmen to shift over to active duty, which were known as Title 10 orders. I desperately wanted to go Title 10. I was young and making good money. In the military, your entire purpose in life is to do one thing, and that worked for me. That direction was exactly what I wanted and needed in my life. I would end up staying Active for ten more years.

SECOND DEPLOYMENT

Shortly after Christmas that year, my friends and I found out about another combat engineering unit going back to Iraq, the 890th. We volunteered and were sent to Fort McCoy, Wisconsin to mobilize. I don't know who thought it was a good idea to send us to an artic hell like Wisconsin in winter so we could deploy to a fiery hell like Iraq in the summer, but apparently I was the idiot.

On this deployment I had the job I was trained for, as a comms NCO. I was part of a PSD/RSD team. PSD stands for Personal Security Detachment and RSD stands for Rapid Security Detail. The PSD team's job was to pull security for the commander when he needed to make visits. For example, we would go out on a mission with the commander for peacekeeping matters, visit other units, or speak to local nationals. RSD's job was to be on call, like a fire department. If somebody got hit or broke down, we would be there as soon as possible to transport them back to the FOB. Everybody else in the 890th worked in route clearance, looking for IEDs. We drove in armored Humvees and MRAPs, and our missions took us into potentially dangerous places like Sadr City.

In theory, my second deployment, beginning in June 2008, should have been much more dangerous than the first. However, the surge was over by 2009 and we had basically won over Iraq. My first deployment was more dangerous because that was the height of the surge, when all the drama was happening.

In movies, it looks like soldiers show up to base after a fight and sit around drinking beers. They get the girls, the medals, and everyone calls them heroes. That couldn't be further from the truth. What they don't show you is all the paperwork. If you shoot a single bullet, you have to fill out mounds of paperwork and after-action review reports. It was a nightmare!

Driving in Iraq was no different to driving through downtown Atlanta, Georgia. There were just as many people and cars. On the second deployment, Tom and I rotated between being the Humvee/ MRAP (that's what we called armored Humvees) driver and the gunner on missions.

The TC (Truck Commander) in the truck was Staff Sergeant Martinez. One day Tom was driving and I was sticking out of the gun turret, with SSG Martinez in the right seat, when we stopped the convoy because of a suspected roadside bomb. We had to wait in the broiling sun, in a traffic jam, for EOD to come blow it up.

Because we were stopped, all the traffic on the road stopped. By the time we got the all-clear, we had waited for about six hours straight, in the middle of July in Iraq, pulling 360 security the whole time because of the risk of attack. We were boiling, cranky, and ill.

That day, our mission had been uneventful. We hadn't had any damage or shot any bullets. We were so close to having an easy mission. Then, sure enough, Tom took out a local vehicle's side mirror along with taking out the side mirror of our own Humvee.

No one spoke. It was like the moment before a tea kettle starts to make that high-pitched whistle. You could feel SSG Martinez about to blow up.

The dumb part about war is all the paperwork that they don't tell you about in the movies. You see, in those films you can blow up anything. Shoot as many rounds as you want and destroy anything and everything you have to achieve the mission and look like Rambo or whoever else you can imagine. In reality, there is paperwork for *everything!* We had been sitting for hours boiling in the sun, and now a broken mirror represented hours' worth of paperwork that had to be done.

SSG Martinez went into some kind of mix between Spanish, English, and ancient Hebrew, laying into Tom over a stupid mirror.

Tom took it, but he was my boy. It was ridiculous and hilarious at the same time. Remember, the military is all about authority and the chain of command. Yet in that moment, after hours baking in mid-July heat like I have never felt down on Route Tampa, I had had enough. Maybe I wanted to defend Ken, or I was simply tired of hearing people complain about a broken mirror on the side of a Humvee. I began a cussing match with SSG Martinez like you would never believe while we drove down the road.

He said a bunch of things in Spanish I didn't understand. I said a bunch of redneck things I am not even sure what they meant. We were driving down the road in a war zone, but the only thing that mattered was who was going to get the last word in with our cussing match. *All* because of a mirror!

SSG Martinez will probably say he won. I will point out that once we got back inside the wire, he hopped out and walked back to our area in a hissy fit.

In the years since, we have become great friends and still laugh about how stupid we were that day.

I defended Tom over that mirror—but the closest person I ever came to stabbing also was Ken. We were running long missions out of Camp Taji. On this particular mission, we had Camp Anaconda on our agenda! Any military person that has been to Iraq knows that if there were a Las Vegas in Iraq, it would have been Camp Anaconda. It was primarily an Air Force FOB, and it had everything you could imagine, including an amazing dining facility (DFAC). Naturally, it was the highlight of everyone's week when we were headed that direction.

Now, we all have things in this life that we simply cannot stand. Lord knows Maury Povich had an entire show dedicated to people who had fears of things like mustard. As for me, I have hated mayonnaise for as long as I can remember. I would rather go to the dentist than eat that which is unholy. In fact, there is a part of me that thinks the Bible translation is not correct in saying the fruit that Adam and Eve ate from the Tree of Knowledge was an apple. It was *mayonnaise!* It is of the devil, and I hate it!

EVEN ON OUR WORST DAYS, AMERICA IS THE GREATEST COUNTRY IN THE WORLD!

Anyway, we hadn't had a decent meal in a long time, and since Anaconda had one of the best DFACs in Iraq, we piled our plates high. They even had an Iraqi version of *Coke*! I had not had a Coke in longer than I could remember. I grabbed one and made my way to the table. I got situated, popped open my Coke and was about to eat the most majestic food I could imagine when I realized I had forgotten utensils. I got back up to grab a fork, returned to my seat, and grabbed the Coke to take that first and oh-so-satisfying swig.

I was met with what felt like curdled milk. I knew immediately what had happened. *There was mayonnaise in my Coke!* Let's just say Jesus kept me from pulling my knife.

Tom was from Boston, and there were very few things that ever would make him rethink his actions. (I once saw Tom take his shirt off in the middle of an argument, ready to fight over the Red Sox.) That day, the fire of a thousand suns filled my eyes, and Tom ever-so-gently slid his Coke to me as a peace offering. He then proceeded to talk about bowel movements, and everything went back to normal.

Ninety-nine percent of the reality of a war zone is like just what I've described: driving down the road, not worried about bombs, and arguing about paperwork we had to fill out because of a busted mirror. Or playing stupid pranks on each other trying to make sense of a world you can never describe correctly. That was my experience, and that was the experience of most people in Iraq. I did more than 200 combat missions, but it was hardly *American Sniper*. Still, we did our jobs well, and I am honored to call everyone I served with family.

My experience in Iraq definitely shaped who I am today. My personality is a mix of mine and the four guys I was around all the time: Eric, Ken, Guppy, and Chausse. By being so close to them, I absorbed several of their character traits into my own, making me who I am now.

I never wanted to be the Special Forces guy; that's not who I am. All I ever wanted to do was contribute. I just wanted to look back at my life and say I did my part. Nobody can say to me that I didn't do it, that I didn't walk out of the wire and do what had to be done.

I believe in my heart that if more Americans had the experiences that we did, they would appreciate our country a lot more. You don't have to be a door-kicker to go over there and realize how good we have it here in America. You don't have to be a Navy SEAL to realize that the places where we fight are terrible places—even on their best days, they are not anywhere close to being as good as the United States. Being there changes your perspective completely.

Even on our worst days, America is the greatest country in the world!

I may not know what it feels like to lose someone on the battlefield, and I thank God for that. I do, however, know what it feels like to leave the safe haven of America and put yourself in a hostile and dangerous position to better the country as a whole. The entire experience made me into a better man, friend, and American.

CHAPTER 4

≡

HOW I MET YOUR MOTHER

Ellisa's and my story starts with a modern-day version of a World War II pen pal correspondence.

Ellisa and I went to elementary school together, but we were not close when we were children. I had a crush on her at the time, but later she barely even remembered we went to school together. The very thing that made me "famous" actually played a huge role in our early relationship. In fact, we might never have become close if it hadn't been for Facebook, which was just becoming a thing in 2008 and 2009, during my second deployment.

During my first deployment, if I wanted to get in touch with someone, I had to write a letter. It took four weeks to arrive in the States, and another four weeks for me to get a reply. By the second deployment, I could go to a communications tent and wait for my fifteen-minute slot on one of the computers that was connected to the internet. I was on Facebook and MySpace, and I spent a lot of time looking up and talking to friends from home, thinking about what I would do when I got back.

One day, on Facebook, I stumbled upon a beautiful girl named Ellisa Carol Vinzant. That was a familiar name, so I sent her a message asking if she was the same Ellisa I knew from elementary school. I had no idea at the time that she had recently been through a bad breakup, which might have helped explain why her reply was so brash. She punched me straight in the mouth, digitally. It's normal for people to connect romantically online now, but back then it was kind of new and still kind of weird. And she definitely thought it was weird. She just about called me a stalker!

Little did she know I was determined. She was beautiful, and I had discovered a connection in our shared past. I kept trying, and she kept being crusty and pretty much giving me the back of the hand.

I eventually wore her down, and we messaged back and forth for a couple of months. Whenever I came back from a mission, I'd check to see if I had a message from her. Sometimes she'd write a lot, and sometimes she'd barely write anything at all. She played hard to get.

I tried to be as smooth as possible. I found a local flower shop near her home and ordered flowers to surprise her. Although she liked the surprise, she was still cautious and surprised that I would send something to where she lived (even though she had told me).

After a few months of this, I went out on a mission and we got stuck in a different location. It wasn't particularly dangerous, just inconvenient. I was gone for a few days, which was unusual for my second deployment. Because Ellisa and I messaged almost daily, she wasn't used to me being gone for any length of time. When I got back to base, I had several messages from her. The first was normal. The second was a little nicer. By the third, she admitted she was getting slightly worried because she hadn't heard from me.

That was the moment I knew…I had her! Getting stuck had been the best thing that could have happened. It changed everything.

STOOD UP

From that point, we started talking more and more. Things began getting serious between us. In October 2008, I had mid-tour leave; I could go home for fifteen days. Ellisa was a student at Mississippi State, so we agreed to meet at Golden Triangle Regional Airport, a tiny, crop-duster-sized airfield in Columbus. No Las Vegas holiday for me; I had a girl to see in Mississippi!

I was awfully nervous as I flew in. The last time I'd seen her in person was in fourth grade. Every military deployment horror story went through my head. I was really afraid that she would stand me up.

And she did!

Well, kind of.

I walked into the terminal, full of butterflies and nerves, wearing my uniform and…nobody. Nobody was there to meet me. "Wow," I thought. "She stood me up."

All right, I told myself. I can rent a car, drive five hours to Alabama and visit my dad for a couple of weeks.

What felt like an eternity was actually five minutes. I was just about to take my walk to Enterprise Rental when I saw her! Ellisa came running into the terminal, carrying big welcome signs. The first word out of her mouth was, "Shoot, can we do it again?" (She didn't really say "shoot," but this is a Christian book and we hadn't quite gotten our lives turned around at that point. You can imagine what was actually said.)

My flight had been a little early. She had been a little late. It was a classic mix-up. But then, everything was fine.

We spent the next two glorious weeks together. I knew that I was going to propose to her in the next few weeks which seems nuts, but it made sense at the time. We knew each other pretty well by then, even if we had been living on opposite sides of the world. On the drive back to the airport, I suggested that she get her own place. She was still in college, living with three roommates. She couldn't afford that. So what did I do? I offered to pay the rent on an apartment of her own, of course!

When I got back to Iraq and told my buddies about my generosity, they were merciless. "You're the dumbest person we ever met," they said. "She's blowing and banging every dude in a house you're paying for, sucker!"

They were just projecting. After all, their dating history could be summed up in any episode of *Jersey Shore*. She saw what I did the way I wanted her to see it; as an example of how committed I was to her.

After a few weeks back in Iraq, I called her dad and asked for his blessing to marry his daughter—it is the Southern way, after all. Once I received his "blessings"—also known as "threats" in most parts of the world—I did what any suave man would do and proposed via webcam. And just like that, we were engaged. We talked on Facebook every chance we could about what our life was going to be like.

I got back to the US at the end of March 2009. Ellisa and I were married a few days later on April 2, 2009, at a courthouse in Alabama. Her parents lived in California, so we waited until her mother and sister could join us and held a big ceremony in June. We were married three months before I even met her dad in person.

Before the ceremony, I went back and printed out all of our Facebook messages to give to her as a wedding present. There were hundreds of pages. Our entire start to our love was right there in black and white. I told you it was a modern-day World War II pen pal story.

HEY, WE'RE PARENTS!

Only a few months into our marriage, I was coming up on the end of my six-year commitment to the Army. Ellisa and I started having serious discussions about whether I'd stay on active duty or get out and go to college. I was twenty-three years old. I had not liked college the first time I tried it, but I thought maybe I should give it another shot. Ellisa was working on her bachelor's degree and I could see the attraction. Luckily for us, God would answer this question for us. Just as we were in the thick of trying to make this *major* decision, *boom*—we found out Ellisa was pregnant. There it was, question answered and decision made. I signed on for six more years of a steady military paycheck.

Our son, Gage, was born on November 18, 2010, and we both turned twenty-four in the two months after his birth. The first time I held my oldest, I was terrified because I didn't want to break him, but I also knew he would be the one who made me better than I ever thought I could be. I didn't realize how big of a journey that would end up being.

We were only just learning to become parents to one child when one day we decided to take Gage to a St. Patrick's day parade. On a dare from Will, who was visiting, Ellisa took a pregnancy test before we went out. You guessed it.

Three months after Gage was born, Ellisa was pregnant with Gunnar; my sons are less than a year apart. "Irish twins," the doctor called it. Ellisa called it being really excited, because she always wanted a big family. I called it *being terrified out of my mind*! Unlike Ellisa, I did not grow up around babies, and I was still learning how to make sure the diaper wasn't on backwards. Yet I found myself a father of two boys, and my heart couldn't have been more full.

I have a picture of us when we found out Gunnar was on the way; we both look white as sheep. We were in shock. Like most young adults who choose to have children, we had absolutely no idea what we were doing as parents. I didn't really know how we were going to make this whole family thing work. There's a common misperception that military men make a lot of money. This isn't true at all, but I signed on for six more years for income security and, more importantly, health insurance.

My paycheck was only around $1,250 every two weeks. That doesn't go very far, especially with a family of four. Ellisa had to get a few credit cards so we could buy diapers for the boys. I will never forget having to use a credit card to buy formula and diapers. I was robbing Peter to pay Paul. I started to feel like a failure. Those were hard money years, and my wife and I started struggling, too.

FAILING AT MARRIAGE

Society has a twisted view of marriage and relationships. You see it in the daily attacks on the modern family. You see it in the messages coming out of the pro-feminist movement, messages that say women don't need men, men don't need women, and children don't need both parents to be okay. We can just do what we want and everything will be fine. Now, I'm not arguing that people can't overcome the cards they're dealt and turn out okay. But women without men, or men without women, or single parent households—that's not the way it's supposed to be. It's just not.

Personally, I never had a good understanding of what marriage should be because my only points of reference were my mom, and that disaster, and my dad, who now has been married five times. Ellisa's parents, on the other hand, are still married today.

In the beginning, we had very different views of how to behave in our relationship. Whenever we hit walls (and we hit many), we didn't know what to do, although I give Ellisa credit for doing things better than I did. She wasn't perfect, but who is? The point is I didn't handle it well and she handled it better, that's for sure.

We had every argument under the sun, from not listening to each other, to not feeling respected, to not having enough sex, to "I'm doing everything in this marriage and you're just coasting." Ellisa and I were two young people trying to grow into real adults. We also both had our own visions of what marriage was "supposed" to be. I was a young guy in the middle of a failing marriage with two kids. I was looking for someone else to make me happy, and that's just not how life works. I wanted Ellisa to be something that she was never supposed to be.

My reaction when we fought was to run away to a bar, drink and threaten divorce. A lot of people have a similar reaction at the first sign that something is wrong. They think, "Well, this ain't working, tell me what you want in the divorce, I'll just pay my child support like my dad did and try this again later."

People in our society are so busy chasing a feeling they don't understand what it means to make a commitment. Initially, I was no exception to this rule. What I see happening in marriages is what I see happening everywhere: every issue, every disagreement, can be boiled down to selfishness and entitlement. Think about it. Fighting, lying, adultery, and drugs can all be attributed to someone being selfish and chasing something for themselves. That's the root principle.

And at the time, as it happens, I was being both selfish *and* feeling entitled.

In the modern world, we're more connected than we've ever been before. We can access information at any point. We can reach out and talk to people across the world whenever we want to. People from lower Alabama can marry people from New York because the world has become more globalized. You have all these different people getting together, *of course* there is going to be disagreements. That's *normal.* The problem is that you can never find someone to make you happy. That's not someone else's job, but a lot of people don't understand that. I certainly didn't. And yet we're teaching the younger generations in America that someone or something can make them happy.

We pushed on for another couple of years. However, the things that we did to "fix" our marriage were simply Band-Aids and were never going to last. When we found out that Ellisa was pregnant with our third child, AnnaGrace, we weren't doing well as a couple at all. It was a dark time in my life—I'm willing to own that. Even though we had a beautiful little girl on the way that would have me wrapped around her finger at first sight, Ellisa and I were practically roommates.

Now that we look back at that time, we realize how many factors were involved. Ellisa was probably suffering postpartum depression. I was a selfish jerk wanting more than I deserved. But here's where I give Ellisa *all* of the credit: she knew what commitment was, even if I didn't. Ellisa never gave up on the idea of our family. She never gave up on me.

For a while, though, I did give up.

When Ellisa was pregnant with AnnaGrace, I walked out and stayed on a friend's couch. I'm not proud of what the man I was then did at all. I look back now with Christ in my life and think, how could I have done that? How horrible of a man I was. The first time it happened, I was out for two weeks. I came back and we had our beautiful daughter, and then we fell into trouble again, so I left for a month. The longest time I was away was about three months. I was still in the Army, but I wasn't on deployment. I was a staff sergeant working as a recruiter, which was more of a nine-to-five job.

Even though I was the miserable one seeking something more, I twisted the problem. I told Ellisa that she and the kids would be better off without me. That was my way of justifying my own selfish actions.

It takes two to mess up a relationship, but I was the one most wrong in my marriage! In the end, I am the one who walked out. Ellisa could have left me, and she would have been right to do so. Yet, she didn't. She never gave up on me. I could blame my bad behavior on my upbringing, or my parents, but in the end that's just excuses. It was me plain and simple. That's another thing we do in this society—find somebody else to blame, instead of taking responsibility for our own actions.

In the end, it doesn't matter what kind of hand you were dealt. What matters is what you do with it.

WHAT LOVE IS

I strongly believe that a common problem within American society is that God is not at the forefront of our marriage and thoughts. Even if you're not a Christian, it's hard to argue with the mentality of Christianity, which is to resist the selfishness within yourself. That's why the name of this book is *America 3:16*.

I once attended a marriage seminar led by a couple who had been married for around fifty years. In those fifty years, they said, they must have fallen in and out of love a thousand times. But they stuck with it. That comment stayed with me.

We aren't properly teaching people what love actually is, and what marriage actually is. Love is a feeling. Love is fleeting. It can go up and down. Marriage is about giving when you don't feel like giving. Marriage is about taking up the mantle when you're tired. Marriage is about choosing the same person every day, whether you love them at that moment or not. If that's not marriage, I don't know what is. Remember what I said earlier?

Sometimes *choosing* someone can mean more than "love" ever could.

While Ellisa and I separated, I still wasn't happy. I would go to the gym and to the movies, but I stopped spending much time with my friends because I wanted to be alone. I began to plan my life after marriage. What's it going to be like? What's it going to look like?

How can I get out of this and get to that new life, because that life over there looks better than my life here? That is the lie that lost people in a marriage begin to believe.

Then I heard something else that stuck with me, from someone I knew. This individual was smart enough to challenge me to see my relationship through a different lens than the one I was using. They didn't ask me about my obligations to Ellisa. At the time, that was the wrong approach. They asked, "Can you look your kids in the eye twenty years from now and say, 'I did absolutely everything I could to stay in your life every day?'"

I STRONGLY BELIEVE THAT A COMMON PROBLEM WITHIN AMERICAN SOCIETY IS THAT GOD IS NOT AT THE FOREFRONT OF OUR MARRIAGE AND THOUGHTS. EVEN IF YOU'RE NOT A CHRISTIAN, IT'S HARD TO ARGUE WITH THE MENTALITY OF CHRISTIANITY, WHICH IS TO RESIST THE SELFISHNESS WITHIN YOURSELF. THAT'S WHY THE NAME OF THIS BOOK IS *AMERICA 3:16.*

That question changed the game for me. It shifted my focus off of myself. The problem wasn't just about Ellisa and me. My relationship with my kids was at stake. We had a family together. Family is forever. Family is all that matters, and somewhere along the way I had forgotten that the Lord had already blessed me with everything I could have ever wanted.

After that, I went into a downward spiral. I became depressed. I would cry and send Ellisa late-night text messages. She would be short with me for obvious reasons, but in the end, she would always just say "come home." Finally, one Wednesday night, all my emotions came to a head. I needed something. I couldn't name it. At this point in my life, my first reaction was not to turn to God. At this point in my life, I *resented* God for all He was putting me through. And church? Well, my church in Mississippi, the First Assembly of God church that had been the focus of my life—they had thrown me out when I was seventeen years old (you'll read more about that in a little bit). They said I wasn't good enough for their church. But even still, God was working in my life.

I had been so angry at that time in my life, and six years later, I was still angry. I was pissed. After all, wasn't this where sinners came to be saved?

Instead of taking my aggression out on the actual people who ran that church, I took it out on God. That left a big void in my life.

That void was why I kept volunteering to go to war. That's why I kept pressing reset and having another child. War and children would take my mind off things for a while. I'd go to war, and it would push that void away. I would come back, and the sense that I was searching for something would reassert itself. After I stopped going to Iraq, I looked to Ellisa to figure out what that "something" was, and to solve it for me. I wanted more sex, more respect, more freedom, more something.

I could find all kinds of reasons I was unhappy except the one in the mirror.

That fateful Wednesday night, I went to church by myself. I'd be lying if I said I remember every word the preacher spoke. Whatever his message, it made an impression. I broke down. After church, I drove straight to our house.

I thought this was something out of left field—Ellisa was never going to see this coming. However, it seemed she had been excepting me. She had prayed for me the entire time I was gone. Unlike me, she had never given up on us. We spoke for hours.

Since that moment, Ellisa and I have made a real effort to put God at the forefront of our marriage and it *truly* has changed everything! Together, we realized that we needed to put God at the center of

SOMETIMES *CHOOSING* SOMEONE CAN MEAN MORE THAN "LOVE" EVER COULD.

our marriage if things were going to work between us. The truth is that God blessed me with my soulmate and the only person who would have been strong and stubborn enough not to give up on me when others would have. I have been blessed for a *very* long time.

Today, instead of asking myself the hard questions, I ask God. When I ask God, "What would You have me do? Would You have me leave my wife?" I get a clear answer. And that answer is why we are together today. When I place my individual focus on God, I have a much better idea of what I should be doing. I am constantly reminding myself, and God is reminding me, that I'm in service to my wife and to my family.

Today, Ellisa and I are the best we've ever been. God was the change for us!

Living this way, we are living a direct reflection of Christianity at its most principled core. Simply put, God is at the front of our marriage. We collectively know that our marriage and our family is nothing without God in it. Through this we have learned that we will never be enough. However, through God we don't have to be, because He is enough. There are an awful lot of elitist jerks in our society who think that everyone else exists to serve them. They think they are entitled to a better man, or a better wife, because they "deserve it." No, you don't. The only things we're entitled to in this country are life, liberty, and the pursuit of happiness. But nobody has ever been *guaranteed* happiness. Think that way and you just

> **"IN THE BEGINNING, I SAVED YOU. SOMEWHERE IN BETWEEN, YOU SAVED ME. IN THE END, WE SAVED EACH OTHER. THE TRUTH, THOUGH, IS THAT GOD SAVED US BOTH."**

set yourself up for failure, and set society up for failure, because that is simply not the way the world is. You can, however, choose joy.

If you follow Christian beliefs, we all deserve nothing but an eternity in Hell. However, through God's grace, we have the opportunity to accept Him and go to Heaven. That's not something we deserve; that's something we get through God's grace. If we don't deserve that kind of fate without God's grace, what makes you think you deserve anything in this life?

This way of thinking, as I said before, is based in selfishness and entitlement. If you deconstruct the arguments in marriage, life, or politics, they're all rooted in selfishness and entitlement—in what people "deserve." That's what's wrong with them.

A big part of the reason I am who I am today is because I realized, through God and through Ellisa and my family, that I can gain a lot more by giving in relationships than by taking. The difference in our marriage today is that we've realized that we don't need to fix each other—that's God's job. God is at the center of our marriage, which is exactly the way it was supposed to be from the start. I have a tattoo that encapsulates our marriage:

"In the beginning, I saved you. Somewhere in between, you saved me. In the end, we saved each other. The truth, though, is that God saved us both."

CHAPTER 5

──────

THE DAILY RANTS

My Facebook videos have collected more than 2 billion views in the last three years. Sometimes I am not sure if I should be proud of that or embarrassed. Yet I would not be where I am today without it. As awesome as other people's "highlight" reels may appear, there are some very negative aspects to social media. To quote Rocky, it ain't all sunshine and rainbows. When people look at other people through the lens of social media—including looking at me or looking at my marriage—they see others they think are amazing and perfect. They ask, why can't my marriage be like that? Why can't my wife be that way? Why can't my husband be that way? Why can't I make that kind of money? Why can't I have my life together like they do?

Social media seems to give you an open window into other people's relationships. But when you try to compare your ordinary life to what you see on social media, you're being ridiculous. You are also setting yourself up for a life of fakery that will never fill the void you are looking to fill. No matter how "real" some people try to be on social media, they are still choosing what to show you, how to show you, and when to show you. Maybe your wife is being mean to you, or you just lost your job, or your husband hasn't gotten out of sweatpants in three days. That's your real life, and it's never going to stand up against the curated life that people like me show you on social media.

You know a little something now about my past, from reading this book. You may think you know me because you've seen me on social media. You might think of me as a random guy who wears sunglasses in his truck and says things to his phone camera. (Honestly, that is probably the most accurate description.)

What you may not realize is that you are looking at the highlight reels. What you may not realize is that, although I try hard to be as real as I can, I still exert a lot of control. This is what I want you to see. This is how I want you to see it. This is what I want you to feel, and when I want you to feel it.

In fact, the only 100 percent "real" people on social media are the ones that aren't on social media at all.

The reality of my family's and my life is nothing special. It may be unique in nature, but "special" is a funny term that I believe only entitled people use. By saying we are "special," instead of just like everyone else, we are saying that we deserve more attention or sympathy. I just don't like it. Everyone has their own story and their own version of trial and tribulation. And we struggle, just like everyone else. As I sit here writing this book, I expect Ellisa is probably mad at me about something. Lord knows, I probably deserve it, for whatever reason. There are certain things I do now,

IN FACT, THE ONLY 100 PERCENT "REAL" PEOPLE ON SOCIAL MEDIA ARE THE ONES THAT AREN'T ON SOCIAL MEDIA AT ALL.

and will do for the rest of my life, that irritate her, and vice versa. The difference, if there is one, is that we realize we don't need to fix the other person.

And the other difference, in terms of how I got famous, is what this chapter is about. I wish I could tell you I'm an entrepreneurial genius or a marketing savant. I wish I could hypnotize you with a really impressive story about how I was in a car wreck and woke up from a coma with all these amazing things to say.

But I can't.

What's *really* the truth? The whole "Dear America" thing was an accident, as most of the best things in business, and life, are. It started out as a joke. I was simply taking advantage of an opportunity to poke fun at things that irritated me and most of the world.

In 2016, I was coming up on the end of my second full tour in the Army. I'd been in almost twelve years, and we had three kids that were no longer babies. They were walking talking little people who reminded me daily that I wasn't as funny as I thought I was. (Kids are awesome that way!) I was working as a recruiter in South Carolina, and I was good at it. Actually, I was great at it. Actually, I was *scary* good at it. I had made Staff Sergeant and was well on my way to Sergeant First Class or E7. I basically talked for a living, talking people into doing things, and I had a knack. In my opinion, the most important skill for an entrepreneur is sales—being able to convince people of things. I attribute a lot of my success in the business world to my military training and recruiter school, where I learned how to talk to people effectively and not fear rejection.

Although I never intended to achieve social media fame, I did have a lot of free time while I was recruiting. I was good at my job, so I got it done quickly. That was the great part of recruiting. If you made your numbers, no one would bother you or try to manage your time for you. So, I created an Instagram page for myself, thinking I could become a voice for *real* America, and be the shining light that is conservative values and Christian ethics.

Actually, no. If you thought that's what I was going to say you couldn't be further from the truth.

The *real* reason I started an Instagram page was because I believed I was going to be America's next top *fitness model*! Stop laughing—I can hear you from where I am writing this book! In 2016, that was all the rage. In fact, fitness athletes were the first experimenters in the "influencer" market. I thought it was my time to shine. It didn't take long for me to learn that I wasn't built enough and wasn't attractive enough to pursue that passion. (I know, that's shocking, isn't it?)

I kept my social media accounts active. I had no idea what I was going to do with them. Some of the higher-ups in the recruiting battalion had encouraged us to look for ways to relate to younger kids better. For that, they wanted us to get on social media more. My recruiting partner, Tanker, and I started making funny videos for Instagram and posting them on our personal accounts. The videos were only fifteen seconds long because that's all you could do on Instagram at the time; we were just having fun. For example, one of our videos showed a black guy and a redneck trying to pick music in the car. When we hit 1,000 views you would have thought we had won a million dollars! Tanker was the first person to tell me, "Hey, you are actually really good at editing videos. You could really do something with this."

A FATEFUL LEFT TURN

I wish I could tell you that I crashed my car and heard a voice tell me to make videos for America. I wish I could say some divine twist of fate led me down the path of righteousness. I can't. In fact, the most asked question I get is, "How did this whole thing get started?" The truth? An old granny ran me off the road.

In July 2016, I was in my government car at the light on Pearman Dairy Road in Anderson, South Carolina, trying to make a left turn. A woman on the other side was making a right. She didn't see what I was doing, so I had to swerve into a ditch to miss her. I love old people. I was raised by my grandparents, after all. However, in that moment, I thought about requiring people over the age of seventy to retake the driving test every year.

I sat there for a moment, ranting about having to fill out a report because now there is a scratch on the G Jet. I don't know what compelled me to do it, but I decided to make a quick video right there about people who don't know how to drive. I sat in my car in a parking lot. I took my uniform off and put my sunglasses on, so I wouldn't have to think about where my eyes were supposed to be looking. I had these *very* out-of-regulation red sunglasses that I wore when no one was looking. It wasn't a brand decision; it was simply what I had at the time. Then I ranted into the camera for the very first time.

I uploaded "What we ALL want to say about Bad Drivers" to Instagram without much thought. I only had about 10,000 followers at the time, which isn't much in the grand scheme of Instagram. Those were the people foolish enough to follow me for my "fitness" expertise who didn't leave after I stopped trying to be America's Next Top Model.

Four weeks went by, and someone suggested in the comments that I upload the video to Facebook. I didn't understand why until I learned that Facebook offered one big advantage over Instagram at the time: videos could be shared. I created a Facebook page and asked my "massive" Instagram following to follow me there. For whatever reason, I decided not to share the bad driving video at that time.

A month after the driving incident, in August, I saw a guy at the gym working out in Spandex leggings without any shorts. He was obviously a CrossFitter. If you ever wondered if someone is a CrossFitter, don't worry, *they will tell you*! As you can imagine, I saw way more than I wanted to see. Dudes who wear spandex leggings with what can only be described as anteaters looking at you while they are doing squats is a crime against humanity, and someone needed to address it! Also, I knew if I heard about one more burpee, I'd scream!

I decided to make another "rant" video, this one about fitness people.

I had about 3,000 followers on my Facebook page when I uploaded my second real rant video onto FB. "What we ALL want to say about Fitness People" was live! There wasn't much movement in the first few hours, so I chalked it up as another failed attempt and decided not to think about it anymore. But on day three, I took a look at the view count: 300,000 views in three days?! I couldn't believe what I was seeing!

I shared the video again and asked all my friends to share the *crap* out of it. Day five rolled around and I had 700,000 views. That quickly went up to 850,000. I got all my friends to share the video *again* because I realized we could break *one million view*s with this thing!

Exactly one week from first posting the video, I sat in the living room with Ellisa, refreshing the page every five minutes, watching the numbers go up. It hit 900,000 views. Then it hit 950,000. Then it hit 999,000. Around 10:30 p.m., one million views! Ellisa and I jumped around the living room. We went viral!

Then we had a weird feeling…what do we do now? However, in that moment, I realized something. I could see the power of the snowball effect. I didn't have any advertising background. I didn't have any plan. But I was starting to think there was some kind of power here.

That being said, I couldn't really comprehend what I was tapping into. The fitness video eventually gained millions more views and brought me 100,000 new followers.

All of my military friends agreed what I was doing was cool. "But there's no way you can do that twice," they said.

Challenge accepted.

My good friend Jake Neele sent me my next video idea. It was about the new debit card chip readers, and how nobody understood how to use them. That did *millions* of views! Next, I uploaded "Bad Drivers." It did *millions*! Then "Bad Drivers Part 2," and on and on we went for the next month.

The truth? I was doing gimmicks, trying to be funny. I talked about anything that annoyed me: bad drivers, bad kids, schools, parents. Whenever I did one, I'd address it to the people I was talking about. I'd say, "Dear Bad Drivers" or "Dear Fitness People." I even did a video about recruiters and made fun of myself! The big social media trend at the time was people lip syncing to songs. I made a video like that and got 10 million views! I'd reached about 160,000 followers by then, but there wasn't any substance to what I was doing, and still no plan.

THANK YOU, COLIN KAEPERNICK

In September 2016, the Colin Kaepernick insanity began. Kaepernick, a backup quarterback for the San Francisco 49ers, remained seated during the playing of the national anthem. Did I mention he was a backup QB? Meaning, he wasn't good enough to be the starter? Get it? Got it? Good, moving on.

At later games, he took a knee only after a veteran told him it would be less disrespectful to take a knee than sit. (Many people misunderstand that entire series of events, thinking a veteran told him it wasn't disrespectful to kneel. That is not even close to the case!) Soon, other players joined him. He said he was protesting police brutality and violence against black Americans. Yet, he never did this before he became a backup QB? Weird, how it happens that way. Was he saying that police brutality was some new thing that began when he was benched, and then he decided to sit for the national anthem? No, I didn't think so either.

For the first time in a long time, I found myself truly angry. Not just irritated about an elderly driver or proper gym etiquette. Yet this time, I had a small audience to say something about it to! I did not think he cared about the black community at all, and I believe his legacy will be one of shame. I believe he was a washed-up backup quarterback searching for relevance and more money. What better way to get noticed from the bench than taking a knee during the national anthem?

I still wasn't overly involved in politics, but I was paying a lot more attention than I had before. Not that I didn't care, I did! It was that politics or current events weren't my life. I watched Kaepernick sit down and I felt angry. I felt *rage*. I felt patriotism for my country and a duty to defend it. Most of all, I felt his action was a blatant slap in the face to every single military veteran who had given their life for his very ability to do what he did.

I decided to make a video talking about Colin Kaepernick. This time, and for the first time, I didn't say "Dear Parents" or "Dear Bad Drivers." I decided to say "Dear America" because I felt for the first time I wasn't speaking to a select group of people. I felt that I was speaking to everyone. Little did I realize that phrase would become who I am and the reason most of you are reading this book.

The title of that rant was, "What We All Want to say About Kneeling for the Anthem." As you can probably guess, it took off! For the first time, I started getting backlash from something I was saying. I got death threats. I was called racist. Anything you can imagine, this video brought it. Clearly, I was talking about something real, which triggered people. There were real emotions coming out. Plenty of people didn't like what I had to say. But many more people did!

I wasn't expecting what happened next.

In the earlier videos, all the comments and messages pretty much read the same way: "Graham, you are hilarious!" and so on. This time, instead of being told I was really funny, or a nut, or even (occasionally) handsome, people left comments like "that's exactly what I think" or "you hit it on the head there" or "you are so right." People even started making suggestions for future videos and rants.

The Kaepernick video changed everything for me. "Holy crap," I thought. "There's a whole group of people who think just like me or feel like I feel." I didn't think people would listen to me or take me seriously. But here they were. *Dear America* had been born!

While all this was going on, I still had to make some decisions about my future. The Army had started to notice the attention and wanted to know by November 1 if I was going to re-up or ETS (End Term of Service) out. After the Kaepernick video blew up, I started to wrestle with my choices. Maybe this whole video thing could be more than I had imagined. Maybe there was more here than people were giving me credit for. It's true that I wasn't making any money at all from the videos. At the time, I didn't know how. But I might be able to figure out how to do that.

I began following the presidential debates and did a video for each one titled, "What We All Want to Say About Presidential Debates." They each got a few million views. I had developed a working system by now. I had broken a code, and the code was working. It was working because I had accidently tapped into what I call *real* America. The people who couldn't say what they felt. I would do it for them! This was exciting, but I still had to figure out what I was going to do.

After I had posted about one of the debates, I was scrolling through the comments when I saw one that froze me: "For those who can't... he'll say it for us!" I must have read that comment over and over again. Let me ask you this: What changes a gimmick into a mission? A purpose! I edited that comment to become my slogan:

"For those who can't...I'll say it for you!"

I sat down with Ellisa and told her I felt like I was onto something, although I didn't know exactly what. "I really think maybe I should get out there and pursue this."

You can probably imagine how that conversation went. There I was, telling my wife that I wanted to give up a guaranteed pension, paycheck, and health insurance in order to make videos for a living. Ellisa has always been incredibly supportive, but at the time she didn't take to my idea very well. That was understandable. On paper, I was making the dumbest decision in the world! In reality, sometimes you have to go with your gut, because you never know how things will turn out. At some point, you have to take the leap!

Think about joining the military, for example. I used to tell kids I was recruiting that if they thought about it too much, they'd never do it. The more you analyze the military, the less likely you are to join. I used this same reasoning to pitch the video idea to my wife. I was selling my wife like I sold kids to join the military.

On November 1, 2016, I had 250,000 followers on social media. And that day I told the military I was going to ETS out. After twelve years, I was done. Ellisa had been willing to listen to me and go along with the plan, even if she hadn't necessarily agreed with my gut feeling. I got no such sympathy from my colleagues. *"You are an idiot,"* they said. *"Are you stupid? You got three kids. What are you going to do, make embarrassing videos for the rest of your life? You're a moron!"*

And so on—plus worse.

At the time those reactions hurt. Now I know they were just trying to protect me. At the end of the day, I know those comments were made from a place of love. Those people closest to me were concerned I was going through a midlife crisis of some kind.

Not two weeks later, in the early hours of November 9, Donald Trump would go on to pull off the biggest underdog win in our country's history. I had spent the evening drinking at a Wild Wings Café in Anderson, South Carolina and watched the results live. I cheered with all of my friends as I watched the country decide to shift into a different direction and Make America Great Again.

Like most of America, I got home about 3 a.m., and I was exhausted the next morning. I didn't intend to make a video. Yet something told me to do it. I didn't have much energy, but I decided to make a video titled, "What We All Want to Say About the Presidential Election." Creatively, it wasn't my best work. Yet until recently that was the biggest video I'd made. In the space of a week, my followers increased to 700,000. That video would be seen by thirty million people! Suddenly, my videos seemed to go everywhere.

PIVOT POINTS

Looking back at my career, I see two distinct pivot points. You have to give credit where credit is due. If Colin Kaepernick had not chosen to act upon his First Amendment rights to disrespect the very men and women who gave their lives so he could do so, the "Graham Allen" that you have come to know never would have come into being. If Donald Trump hadn't won the election, I never would've made the presidential election video. And without *that* video, nothing else would've taken off in the way it did.

From a technical perspective, that presidential election video was the first time I hit an issue the minute it happened. I believe my video took off because I was responding to big issues in real time, within twenty-four hours of something happening. I was onto something, and that's how my business model was born.

I had figured out how to make the videos take off, but I had to figure out how to make money. It was time to hustle. I had some followers, so I started reaching out to companies for potential sponsorships. Most companies, though, had not figured out the influencer market yet. After much work, I got my first sponsorship: $3,500 a month for six months. That was it—all the money I had coming in, even with 700,000 followers. Not bad, but for a family of five and with no long-term guarantee. I had some work to do!

I started grinding it out. I made videos all the time, aiming for two a week while trying to meet anyone and everyone I could who might just listen to me, yet alone sponsor me.

I shot the videos in my truck. I was traveling a lot at the time, which was great for word-of-mouth promotion. I'd call companies and introduce myself. I'd drive around for meetings and in-person talks. I'd pay my own way to events like SHOT Show in Las Vegas. I slept on floors. I slept on RV couches. I went anywhere and everywhere people would let me. As I began to get sponsors, I asked them to get me into events I couldn't otherwise get into. I'd meet Second Amendment companies, veteran companies, and patriotic companies. I was elbowing my way into a world I didn't really know or understand, but I had to figure it out, and I knew I didn't have much time.

Up until this point our whole marriage had revolved around military life. We got a check on the first and the fifteenth of the month. I had very clear duties, responsibilities, and a schedule. Now, suddenly, everything was hustle-and-grind: "Honey, I gotta go, I'll be back in a week or so, maybe I'll grab some sponsors." There was no fixed schedule, no guaranteed money, no guaranteed anything. There were some cool days, sure, but there were some days that really sucked, too. Ellisa doesn't get enough credit for helping to create this business. Without her being who she is, doing the hard job of keeping the family running while I went off to try and create something, all of this wouldn't have happened.

For the first year, I repeated a process which I knew worked for making videos about relevant topics. Videos like "What we ALL Want to Say about Election Protesting," and teachers, and parenting, and North Korea, and so on. With all that traveling, I was usually gone for about three weeks a month. This was a strain on my family, and it took a lot of adjustment. Some days were great and other days were a real struggle. To say that there were times I doubted myself would be an understatement. It's easy to sit back and say, "Oh yeah, of course I should have done that," or "That was a great idea!" But no one had heard of The Daily Rants. I was creating it.

Slowly but surely, we were moving the needle. We were growing at a rate that nobody else was in the social media space I occupied. Between August 2016 to the end of January 2017, we reached a million followers. From January 2017 to October 2017, we got another million. And in that first year, all of the videos I made collected over a billion views. By October, less than a year in, I had 2.1 million followers across my platforms. After I landed my first sponsor, I got another one within about thirty days. In the next thirty days, I got another. Then I got a deal big enough that we could cover rent and both car payments on that deal alone. In about eight months, I landed my first major deal.

By this time, Ellisa was feeling much better about the situation. I wasn't a millionaire, but things were finally moving in a positive direction. I had a little office, and a lot of people would have left what I'd built alone and let it run. Yet anyone who knows me well will tell you I don't stay satisfied for very long. I thought, "It's time to evolve this."

You might look at that growth—which was faster than anyone else in my space—and think, gee, that's pretty good, why change things?

But I always look at things and see what's missing. What can we do better, how can we mature, how can we grow past where we are? I had learned that most people in social media flame out. They're one-hit wonders. I knew I had to keep moving fast or I was going to fail.

I watched what other people were doing. I studied successful people and learned *why* they were successful. I studied people whose channels had died off and learned *why* that happened. Originality is important, but you can't always manufacture it. What could I do right, and what should I avoid doing that was wrong?

I noticed that a lot of social media personalities started going after quick money. They created their own T-shirt lines, for example. Or companies would reach out to people with large engagements and ask them to share articles from the company's page, which would garner website traffic for the company. The individual would get paid "x" number of cents per click. Initially, people would make $50,000 a month doing that but, soon enough, they would cannibalize their audience. Facebook didn't like this either and would kill their engagement with algorithms, thus ending that person's business.

I saw that those ads, links, or articles that brought easy money were actually hurting people, not helping them. It's like they were pitchers who were trying other things that were messing up their fastball. If you can't throw a fastball, you're not a pitcher anymore. I couldn't mess with my fastball. I couldn't go down that easy-money route.

At the same time, I knew I had to change. Well, change may be a bad word. I had to evolve and mature. Otherwise I'd end up like one of those child actors who grows up and doesn't bring the audience along with him. I had to figure all this out, and fast. I couldn't be *The Daily Rants* guy forever. That's how people had known me for a while, and it worked well while it lasted. But I knew I needed to shed that persona to avoid being a gimmick forever.

I stopped being *The Daily Rants* guy because I realized it was a gimmick. I wanted to be Graham Allen. I wanted to be able to keep doing what I was doing, but I also wanted more. I wanted to be able to talk about serious topics. I wanted to move into long form content. Most importantly, I wanted my audience to grow with me. If you've been following my videos for a while, you've seen that shift—and that's why it happened.

DEAR TV NETWORK...

Even though we were growing, it's not like opportunities were falling in my lap. Quite the opposite. I got my TV show, for instance, by nothing but old-school cold calling.

Here's how that happened.

I had always been a fan of Steven Crowder, who had the show *Louder with Crowder*. He worked with a network called CRTV, Conservative Review Television. I looked up to him, but I also thought "I can do that!" When I browsed CRTV's website, I was shocked to discover there was no "Request your own TV show" button.

Crazy, right?

My only evident option was to send a message through the "Contact Us" link on their page, the place where people cancel their subscriptions or complain that their service isn't working. I typed out an email introducing myself, explaining that I had one of the fastest growing social media channels in the country, and that I had a great idea for a TV show.

Shockingly, they didn't write back.

So I just kept grinding. I worked hard through November and December, constantly aware that I had an expiration date on *The Daily Rants*. I knew I needed my brand to become Graham Allen somehow. If I didn't, my whole business would die out. The key to business is being aware. So many people get something that works and don't realize you have to keep working at it to keep it working. That wasn't going to be me.

One day in January, I get an email from someone calling himself the "President of CRTV." I was convinced it was a scam.

Wrong!

"Hi," the email read. "My name is Carroll, and I am the president of CRTV."

For real?

Yep. It turned out he received my email in October and had been watching me for the last three months.

Lesson learned: just because you don't receive an answer straight away doesn't mean nobody's watching.

When I pitched my idea to Carroll, he said that CRTV could get on board. It was happening—I was getting my own show!

Originally, I thought I'd call the show *The Daily Rant with Graham Allen*. I was set on that concept, until someone suggested it might be a bit too similar to what I was already doing.

At the time, I was a huge fan of *Man v. Food*, which all began with Adam Richman. As the show became more successful, it grew into *Man v. Food Nation*. It still had the same premise, but he included fans as well. I loved the idea of giving the concept back to the people, in the same way that the Founding Fathers gave America back to the people.

They didn't have to do that, but they did because it was the right thing to do. Adam Richman didn't have to give his concept back to his audience, but he did it. That worked for me.

That's where the idea of *Rant Nation* came from. I was really passionate about including everybody. We could take it on the road and travel between different locations. From the first pitch, *Rant Nation* stuck.

All of this approval from the network didn't mean I was home free. I had to prove myself. They gave me a very small amount of money in the grand scheme of TV show production and said, "Make a pilot."

Fifteen thousand isn't a lot of money for a TV pilot. I found a production company associated with Duck Dynasty, and through them found Phil Robertson's nephew, Elliott Newman, who had started Restoration Productions. They were willing to take a chance with me.

Shooting the first pilot was frugal, to say the least. Since CRTV's main studio was located in Washington, D.C., we went there to shoot, which saved money on studio rental. I'd never been in such a situation, but I was going to make the most of it.

We converted their news studio as best we could to make it look like Rant Nation—except Rant Nation wasn't a thing yet. It was all in my head. We did the best we could to make what was in my head happen in two days with $15,000. I ended up sitting at a random wooden table, draped a flag in the back with our Rant Nation logo, and that was about it.

My friend, the comedian Chad Prather, dropped everything and flew to D.C. to film with me. That was a little payback to him for all he'd done for me. When I started making videos, Chad was already famous on the internet. He was one of the only people at the time who was willing to give me real advice. (Chad met Carroll when he came to D.C. and later ended up getting his own show on BlazeTV when the networks merged. It's funny how things work out.)

The awkward part was that we filmed the pilot in February but knew it wouldn't launch until the middle of March. We needed to figure out what to talk about that could be somewhat timeless. Chad and I started talking about the church and modern kids. Nothing was particularly scripted, but I did have bullet points about certain topics. Because my content is based on people's opinions, I leave a lot of room for improvisation. Every topic is shaped by our opinions, value systems, and worldviews.

Filming the pilot was different from anything I'd done before. I was used to being by myself. If I screwed up by myself, nobody would have to know. Suddenly, I was sitting in front of a group of people who were relying on me to get it right. It was a steep learning curve.

To this day, I hate that first episode. Like most pilots, it just wasn't very good. (Go back and look at the pilots of your favorite TV shows—you'll probably see they aren't very good, either.)

Things were moving fast. Carroll and I had begun talking about the show in January 2018. We filmed the pilot episode on February 27. On March 15, it launched on the network.

After we launched, we had to wait. That was the scary part. CRTV is a subscription network. Whether we got a contract beyond the pilot depended on how many subscriptions the network sold in the two weeks after we aired. Subscriptions (which were for all of CRTV's programming) cost $130 apiece, which is real money. And we needed to sell several thousand subscriptions for the network to realize I was onto something.

I did what I could. I announced the show to my audience, which added more pressure. The show wasn't a secret anymore. If it didn't get picked up, everyone would know about my failure.

But by April, we knew we were in—and not just for a year. The subscription sales were so good that CRTV gave us a three-year contract right away! Suddenly, we were committed to making ninety-six shows a season, at a rate of two episodes per week.

ON AIR

And just like that, I had a TV show—and an awful lot of work to do. A preacher once said, "We all want blessings in our life, but then complain about the work associated with those blessings." Turns out a TV Show is *hard* work. Especially when you are not only the one having to be in front of the camera, you are also the one who has to come up with all the ideas.

CRTV offered to build me a studio anywhere I wanted. They committed hundreds of thousands of dollars to it, and we began to build a team.

Anywhere I wanted? That was an interesting question. It really got me thinking.

I tend to make decisions with my gut, and that's worked out pretty well for me so far.

I had a gut feeling that I needed to go home and take the studio back to Mississippi. Not California. Not New York. You see, when most people see success, they start trying to "fit in." They move to where they think things are happening and can play their part. I didn't want to be that way. Mississippi. At first, everyone thought I was crazy. When I could go anywhere, why would I want to go back to Mississippi?

I'll tell you why.

To this day, I still film my videos in my car on my phone, because I want people to understand that I'm just like them. I knew we couldn't afford to lose that connection.

"Look," I said, "people look at us and listen to us because I'm the guy who says what other people want to say but they can't. If we go too big, too fast, we're going to lose those people. It's time to go home. We need to tell everybody, too, that we're going to go home. And then we go to the middle of Mississippi and do things my way."

Off we went, back to Lowndes County, Mississippi, where I was born and raised and where my entire existence had fallen apart. From the kid with the broken childhood, I was now a hometown hero with a TV show. We moved my entire family and our film crew to Nowhere, Mississippi. There were five of us in production, and it was us against the world. That was the way we liked it.

As the show grew, we created a social media page for it. It took me almost two years to hit two million followers on the Graham Allen page. The *Rant Nation* page was a different story; we hit two million followers in six months and became CRTV's most followed show. One of my videos alone got 1.8 million shares and over 130 million views. We did a billion views in ten months!

To put it bluntly, we were absolutely killing it.

I still don't know exactly why people watch what we do, but I can tell you that God had a hand in all of it. One thing that I love about this work is being involved in the entire process, from the way everything looks to the titles and the cut scenes. A lot of old-school, trailblazing TV hosts have assistants that do everything for them.

They walk in and do the show. Some people never even watch the episode after it airs. I've never been like that. I never wanted anyone to touch the set or book a guest without me.

Equally, I pay attention to people's comments. I pay attention to what's trending. I get involved in politics and culture. I'm all about faith, freedom, religion, military, and Jesus. I am not the best. That is for sure. However, if you made a list of the top fifty conservative voices right now, I'm on that list. I think of myself as more cultural than political, although they blend together. I talk about the things I feel deeply and make a real effort to remain true to the reasons my audience started watching me in the first place.

The old-school way is to take a diamond in the rough and put them on a big network to create a following around them. Many *massive* musical artists have been formed the same way. A label signs five pimply-faced kids, they dye their hair, give them some Oxy 10 and turn them into NSYNC. It's a machine. These days, if a band doesn't have a following or thousands of sales and downloads, they won't even get a meeting with anyone.

The same used to happen in the world of commentators and pundits. Today, you've got to have a following first. There's no longer a path for the person who gets on FOX News as a field reporter and works their way up. In order to get a conversation about having a platform like a TV show, you need to prove that there's something about you for people to latch onto. This is the new wave. In my case, I accidentally tapped into it. My job is to hang onto it and grow it. My audience is why I am where I am.

PODCAST EXPANSION

The success of *Rant Nation* led to my next big idea: a podcast.

As I said, I'm always looking for how to evolve, particularly when things are going well. We'd set up in Mississippi and the show was doing great. We started talking about contract extensions, more money, and bigger productions. I'm in politics and culture, but I'm not just politics or culture. I'm a TV personality, but I'm also a normal person. People know me, but it's hard to pinpoint exactly who I am. I love being in this space.

I knew we had more to give, and I always want to get better at what I'm doing. How could I reach more people?

Although the show was successful, it is behind a paywall at CRTV. That inherently limits the audience. What intrigued me about a podcast is that it's free. It's also much longer, which gave me room to say and do more.

A *Rant Nation* episode, without commercials, is fifteen to twenty minutes long. A podcast can run much longer. Nobody really believed I could go long-form, but I had a feeling that I could. I wanted to call my podcast *Dear America*. That was my original brand, and it could encompass *The Daily Rants* and the *Rant Nation* TV show.

By the spring of 2019, I was in a little different position at CRTV. First, the network had merged with BlazeTV (and taken that name), so I was talking both to Carroll and Martin, who were now co-presidents of BlazeTV. Second, I wasn't an unknown quantity anymore. I was a success, at least at that network. That give me a little leverage as I got on conference calls to pitch my podcast idea.

It was an uphill battle. I had some very clear ideas. I wanted to bring my producer in front of a microphone. He has a very different personality than me; he's very even-keeled. And I wanted Ellisa to be a regular part of the show, because nobody will stand up to me the way that Ellisa will. I knew that Ellisa would argue with me until the ends of the Earth when she disagreed, which was important.

Nobody at the network really saw where I was coming from. First of all, they didn't like *Dear America*. They wanted it to be *The Graham Allen Show*.

"That's just dumb," I said. "I'm not doing that."

"How about the *Dear America Podcast with Graham Allen*?"

"I'm not saying that. I'm not saying, 'What's going on, everyone? I'm Graham Allen, and welcome to *Dear America Podcast with Graham Allen*.' It's not going to work. It's not me."

They didn't see the value of adding other people either. "Why not keep it simple," they said, "do it like Ben Shapiro, just talking into a microphone?"

Nope.

Although they were too polite to say so directly, everyone thought I'd completely lost my mind. They didn't want to come out and call me a moron, but that's what they were thinking.

I knew I had a pretty good chance of getting my way, because we were riding on success, and that success was based on my talent and my gut. We weren't going to be better than everyone else by being exactly like everyone else.

Slowly but surely, the producers started coming around to the idea of having other people on the show, but there was *a lot* of back and forth. We argued about almost everything. Finally, I convinced them to let me do it my way. If it didn't work, I'd admit all of my mistakes with my tail tucked between my legs.

We launched the podcast in June 2019, producing just one episode a week. We didn't think the podcast would fail, but we had no idea what would happen next. The podcast debuted at number eleven in the world within three days of its release! Now, we remain one of the top 200 podcasts in the world.

Bottom line: the podcast has been our most successful venture to date. Whenever I meet people now, they can't stop talking about the podcast; it's like I've never done anything else. Of course, the reason the podcast is so successful is because we took everything that had worked for us before and made it even better.

I still go off on tangents. I still get worked up and carried away, but I didn't want to be the rant guy. I wanted to be myself, Graham Allen, and incorporate two other real people. We don't always agree on everything which creates a really cool atmosphere.

My ultimate goal is to just be different. We're trying to transcend beyond politics. Our guests have included the likes of Skillet, Candace Owens, Congressman Dan Crenshaw, and even the guys from

Floribama Shore, the number one show on MTV. I do talk about politics a lot, but I also try to do it in a way that doesn't alienate someone who isn't as interested as others.

WHAT'S THE POINT OF ALL THIS?

That's how, in three short years, I went from a guy yelling at his phone in a car to being the public "Graham Allen" so many people now know.

That's how it happened—but why do I do it? Why do I put myself out there, and take the abuse that comes with this kind of public position? What am I trying to accomplish?

Think of me as someone who loves America and wants to help everyone remember how blessed we are to be in this country. I want to ensure that we're leaving our kids a better America than the one we grew up in. Nowadays, it feels like everyone is trying to make everyone happy. That was never the point of America. A better America doesn't mean an easier America. The point is to have opportunity.

I hope that the people who have watched me from the start are still enjoying my content. Although we've matured, we're still the same people we always have been. Fortunately, the vast majority of my audience love the things I stand for today, even if I don't know exactly why they latch onto me rather than anyone else. Don't get me wrong, there are a lot of people who dislike me. That's fine. I don't need everyone to love me. I just need to know who I am and do what I can with that.

I'm not Charlie Kirk or Candace Owens or Ben Shapiro. I'm Graham Allen. All I want is to be the best version of me that I possibly can. I'm not special. I wasn't this amazing person in the military. I'm not the best person in the world. As long as I remain true to who I am and what I believe, to being authentic, I feel that our audience will continue to grow. Today, one of my biggest challenges is to stay vigilant throughout the process while also moving towards the next big thing. We did 130 million views last week? Cool—what's next?

Now that you know how we got here, now that you know what shaped the person you see on the internet or TV every day, let me take you behind the scenes to what I see happening to our country on a daily basis. We are in a fight for our future. Let me show you what I mean.

FAITH

I would be nothing without the love and grace of God. I have learned in my life that I deserve nothing, and it is only through His grace that I have any of the blessings that I have within my life. My faith is the fundamental key that holds my life together.

CHAPTER 6

TOXIC MASCULINITY

When I started making videos a few years ago, I was definitely trying to be funny—I focused on being funny. I was very orchestrated and intentional to that end, although I didn't have a plan beyond being funny. With my current audience, I feel an obligation to counteract the false narratives being put out into the world, which aren't always political. For example, not long ago the actor Charlize Theron announced that her seven-year-old son has decided to become a girl. No, he hasn't. Charlize Theron, as an adult, has been able to make that adult decision for him. I have nothing against transgender people when they're able to make an adult decision for themselves. I don't believe in it. However, they are Americans. But let's be clear: she decided that for him.

That's the kind of thing I speak about these days.

People often tell me that my videos have become a way for them to say what they want to say without actually saying it. (After all, that's my slogan!) Many of them are afraid of upsetting other people with what they know to be true to their own values and morals. By sharing my videos, they can express their own beliefs too. I can make a video, and they can share it, telling people, "take a look at this" as a way of showing how they feel, too. I take all the heat for it, and they have a way to express how they feel.

For example, I took a stand that the truest kind of toxic masculinity is no masculinity at all. We need real men to raise up young men for the future. Real men who respect women, work hard, stand up for the unborn, love God, and love this country. It really is that simple.

I made this point in response to an ad that Gillette ran in January 2019. And man, did I step in it! A lot of people want to be "famous," yet what they don't realize is when you put yourself in that situation, people will love you, but people also will hate you! I have learned the hard way that hate has no boundaries. A single photo and a one-line caption went global! What I did caused me and my family a lot of pain and emotional hurt, but it also showed the power that I and the silent majority of Americans have.

A DANGEROUS NARRATIVE

If you look up the word "toxic" in the dictionary you'll find synonyms such as poisonous, venomous, virulent, noxious, dangerous, destructive, harmful, unsafe, malignant, injurious, pestilential, pernicious, and environmentally unfriendly.

If you look up the word "masculinity" you'll find synonyms such as virility, manliness, maleness, vigor, strength, muscularity, ruggedness, toughness, robustness.

The term "toxic masculinity" took a while to evolve, but it's been hinted at in the culture for years. Look back at the popular sitcoms of the late 90s and early 2000s, such as *Roseanne*. They had a similar tone and premise: pretty much all of them featured a spunky wife and a dumb husband who provides some comic relief. All propagate an illusion of a moronic husband the wife has to put up with. Don't get me wrong, I love some of these sitcoms. *Kings of Queens* is my favorite. But the more I watch them now, the more I notice the false narrative they create about men and women in society: men are morons and women save the day.

When *Will and Grace* came out, it was the first time a show had made space for the LGBTQ community. I've got no problem with that, but it was another step toward redefining masculinity. Jump to the 2010s, and you could really see something change in the culture. The #MeToo movement began to take shape, which started off as good, but has inherent problems too.

I want to be clear: I love women. Women are amazing. None of us would be on this planet if it weren't for women. I admire their strength and power. Feminism in its truest form—empowering women to be strong and independent—could have been a really good thing. Unfortunately, we have moved away from that kind of feminism to a feminism that is based on one thing: complete and total hatred of men! Feminism is now about breaking men down. More specifically and more horrifically, men are the problem.

Feminism today is about defining men as the enemy of society.

The #MeToo movement, which has grown out of feminism, is particularly insidious. Now don't get me wrong, Women need to speak up about rape and sexual abuse, and good men need to support them when they do! The men who commit heinous acts deserve to be prosecuted to the full extent of the law. Don't misunderstand me here: there is *no place* in society for sexual assault perpetrators or rapists. I wholeheartedly support prosecution of Kevin Spacey, Harvey Weinstein, and Matt Lauer.

However, like many good ideas, even the #MeToo movement has started to shift our principles as Americans so that men seem like the worst possible humans within our society. I saw this early when #MeToo shifted into #BelieveHer. Simply put, just "believing" someone over evidence is not how our system works or is supposed to work.

 In America, if you're accused of something, you're innocent until you're proven guilty. You have every right to defend yourself and not be cast out of society until we get to the bottom of things. To see how our culture has twisted this, just look at two high-profile events: the O.J. Simpson trial and the Brett Kavanaugh Supreme Court hearings.

Think back to the O.J. Simpson trial in the mid-90s. Even though most people believed that O.J. was guilty, the court proceedings still went on as they were supposed to. His crimes needed to be proven, and when they weren't, he was set free.

Brett Kavanaugh's hearing was very different; he had to fight to prove that he *didn't* do what he was accused of. He was guilty until proven innocent. His confirmation hearings were one of the most horrific instances of slander in recent memory. To say that they will be written and talked about for the rest of our lives is an understatement. This is the exact opposite of the fundamental framework of our judicial system.

The Left and the mainstream media sought to destroy a man and his family because they knew he would swing the power in the Supreme Court to a more conservative way of thinking. It happened in front of our very eyes. All of us stood back and watched the ridiculously obvious political game being played. We are told now to "believe her" when a woman makes an accusation. That leads to horrific trouble. To simply believe, and not to question, does no one any good of any kind. We might as well bring back the Salem Witch Trials—after all, the accusations weren't true, but they were believed.

Conservatives looked at the Kavanaugh hearings and finally stood up. We knew that this was just wrong, and we won that fight.

Even then, there was a cost. Brett Kavanaugh is never going to be seen the same way by society. You can't come back from a rape accusation, even if you are innocent. Your reputation is damaged forever.

Somewhere along the way on this journey toward toxic masculinity, our understanding of rape became blurred. Rape is a very, very serious thing. But the #MeToo movement and #BelieveHer have tried to change the meaning of what rape even is. I recently saw a tweet that said lying for sex is rape. Really? Have we become so confused between our emotions and facts that we have forgotten the actual definition of rape?

If I tell you I make a million dollars a year, and you have sex with me, and then find out I only make $50,000, is that rape? Or if a woman forgets to tell me that she has a three-year-old child at home, and we have sex, is that rape? That sounds ridiculous, doesn't it? But it's what happens when we boil everything down to a victim mentality and the idea that men are bad.

Look at what happened to Aziz Ansari. By opening up about a bad date for the purposes of comedy, he opened himself up to sexual assault allegations, which shouldn't be the case.

Feminism isn't about men being bad. Feminism is about women being equal and having power. Women need to speak up about this!

THE GILLETTE AD

By the time January 2019 rolled around, four months after Kavanaugh was sworn onto the Supreme Court, there was a change in the air. People were saying that conventional masculinity had become toxic.

You very well may have seen the Gillette commercial about toxic masculinity. If you haven't, I recommend you find it and see what you think. The ad has a dark undertone throughout. It shows mindless men repeating in unison that "boys will be boys," young boys fighting at a backyard cookout, men making sexual advances on women, and it strongly suggests that the way men behave, and what they accept in others, is a problem.

I first saw the ad at the studio in Columbus. We were renting out the old Graham Roofing building, where we'd built a little recording studio to film *Rant Nation*. We didn't even have cable TV there, which is kind of funny when you consider I'm in the media business. It is dark, with no windows, no logos, nothing to proclaim that we were getting almost 10 million viewers a day. It felt kind of like a prison to me, but it was an improvement over filming in my beat-up F-150. We operated every day like it was us against the world, and we were winning.

We did have internet in the building, and that's how I first saw the ad. I saw it was trending but didn't know what it was, so I stuck my head in my producer's office and we watched it together on YouTube.

Eventually a million people *disliked* that video, and I was one of them.

I felt upset, though I couldn't immediately say exactly why. I held off on responding until I knew what I wanted to say. After all, lots of people were asking, "How can you be upset that it says you should treat people better?" I agree—no one can argue with that. But there was something else going on.

I turned it over in my mind until I decided that it was the undertone of the commercial that bothered me, because it implied that this is the undertone in our society. The ad, and Gillette, wanted us to believe that the younger generation was in charge of saving themselves from the current generation of misogynists and rapists that were ruining the country. If you didn't know better, you'd come away from that ad thinking that men are the root of all the problems within American society—that the majority of men tolerate or even promote bullying, homophobia, and sexual assault. This is not simply dishonest; it is a blatant lie.

Let's remember, the majority of men are not rapists. The majority of men understand that women deserve respect. The majority of men do not support bullying or condone acts of hate or violence. The majority of men *love women*. We know our mamas run the house 90 percent of the time. Real men respect women. Real men know the difference between yes and no. Real men defend those who are less powerful and use their strength to lift them up. Real men are what we need.

So what was Gillette trying to say? I believe they were testing the waters, trying to see how far the line had shifted against traditional manhood.

Just because there are bad apples, that doesn't mean all men are bad. That's like saying all women are good. You see the same criticism of America's police officers, who are some of the bravest men and women in our country. The actions of a few officers have damaged the reputation of an entire police community, which is made up of brave men and women who put on the badge every day to go out and protect people who may hate them. Saying that all police officers are bad, or all men are bad, is as ridiculous as saying all women are bad. Are there bad women? Of course. Are all women bad? Of course not!

So that much was bothering me about the Gillette ad for sure.

I also got to thinking about double standards.

One of my favorite country music songs is Chris Kane's *The House Rules*, about the unwritten rules in a man's favorite bar. The seventh rule is that men should not touch women, but women "can grab whatever they want to." In my opinion, this is a direct reflection of our double standards in society. A man can't get drunk in a bar and grab a woman—that makes him some kind of sexual offender. But a woman doing the same is strong, independent, and going after what she wants. Really?

This sort of double standard is running rampant in our society. Here's another example: If a woman were to see a straight man's penis in an office, this would be considered sexual assault. But if a ten-year-old girl were to see a man's penis in a girls' bathroom because he identifies as a woman, this is tolerance? If that's not a double standard, I don't know what is.

To me, the current situation in society is a broad attack on hetero-sexual men, and the Gillette ad crystallized that. As I was thinking about why that ad bothered me, I realized that today, the most scru-tinized and criticized group within our society is straight, white, Christian males.

And that I simply could not let stand.

LOCKER ROOM BRILLIANCE

Most of my best ideas come when I'm at the gym, and this time was no different. A couple days after watching the Gillette ad, I went and worked out at the gym. I took a shower, thinking about what I wanted to say in response. For the first time, I felt like a video wasn't the way forward. I wanted to post a picture instead. That was all—just a single image.

The photo I decided to post was of me, my two sons, and my daughter. Many people claimed the photo was staged for my response to Gillette, but it wasn't. It was taken months before. The photo was inspired by the stereotypical old Southern ideal of a dad and sons having guns to protect the girl of the family. We stood in a cotton field across the street from our house. It was one of about 300 we had taken during a family photo session two months earlier, some of which were in my phone.

As we were taking the photos, I decided to incorporate the three guns I happened to have in my truck that day: a shotgun, a Shield .45, and a Daniel Defense 7.62 AR rifle. Had I known how important that photo would become, I would have brought out my entire gun collection. The point of the photo was to create an image of men protecting the girl in the center—the kind of photo a dad shows her first date, many years down the road. We took it and I forgot about it until I scrolled through my phone that day in January.

Sitting in the locker room, I uploaded the picture to Instagram, Facebook and Twitter with a simple caption:

"Practicing our toxic masculinity." Hey, Gillette, does this offend you?

Uploading that picture was definitely the most powerful thing I did that day, but I didn't know it at the time. I went straight to the set to shoot *Rant Nation*. I didn't even look at my phone until we were done filming..

In a few hours, that photo had gone everywhere. People had Photoshopped it, too, and some of the results were pretty funny—for instance, someone took the guns out of the picture and replaced them with Gillette razors. Among the more popular criticisms was a comment from a girl who wrote, "Gillette says treat people better…this guy: you can't take our GUNS!"

Of course, there were no guns in the Gillette ad. I chose to include guns in my response because I knew what Gillette meant by their ad. I also was fairly certain that the people who created the commercial would consider guns "toxic." That's why I wish I had added the word "too" to my post: "Hey, Gillette, does this offend you too?"

When I checked my email later the next day, I saw that Yahoo! had been trying to reach me. They wanted to run a story on my photo within the hour and were asking if I wanted to comment. My number one rule in responding to the press is to not make a quick statement because they have some kind of deadline. That email from Yahoo! was the first time a predominantly left-leaning news outlet had reached out to me. I didn't respond. I just let them say whatever they wanted to say and went about my business. Yahoo! Lifestyle put a story up at three o'clock that afternoon. It wasn't a slam, it wasn't great. But it started to get a lot of attention.

From there, it took off! People all around the world took the photo and continued to share it and manipulate it.

Any press is good press; it comes with the territory. If I'm not making somebody mad, chances are I'm not doing my job properly. If you want to be famous, you had better be prepared for a portion of people to hate you. However, the day after the article was published, things got really heated. Because the Yahoo! Lifestyle article was doing so well, Yahoo! moved it to the front page of their website. Lots of other outlets began running it too, in places around Europe and Australia.

All of a sudden, that picture was *everywhere*. A good news story lasts seventy-two hours. A big news story lasts a week. Ours definitely fit into the latter category. People referred to it as "the picture seen 'round the world."

"Gun-Happy Family Is Joining the Resistance against Gillette," read one headline. Another said, "Dad and His Children Pose for Family Photo Carrying Guns: Hey Gillette, Does This Offend You?" The criticism got so intense that I considered deleting the picture entirely, and we talked about that as a team. These days, everybody wants to put you out of business or force you to retract any statement you make. I decided to stand up to the apologetic cancel culture that exists in society today.

I decided against taking the picture down because I didn't care what people assumed about me. I know I'm not a racist or misogynistic person. The people who hated me would hate me no matter what I did or said.

For about a week, we were portrayed as the most racist, misogynistic, bigoted family in America. This affected me more than it normally would because my children were involved. I can deal with negative press about myself, but this was the first time I made a decision which affected my kids. These days, if we disagree culturally or politically, nothing is off limits any longer. Typically critics will go after the softest targets, such as children. It's one thing to have people hate me. It's another thing to have them go after my children. Their faces were plastered everywhere, and nobody was bothering to blur them out.

Trust me, we heard it all after that. I was accused of being racist because we were subtle enough to stand in a cotton field. In my opinion, this is giving me way more credit than I'm due. We just walked across the street. I mean, we lived in Mississippi—there's a lot of cotton around. I was accused of child abuse, because of the guns. I was accused of being sexist, because my four-year-old daughter was the only person in the picture *without* a gun. It was the full trifecta: racist, sexist child abuser. I suppose if I'd been wearing an "I Hate Gays" T-shirt it would have been the photo of the year for some people. For a solid week I represented the worst of American society.

If I can paraphrase Forrest Gump, a racist is as a racist does. I've learned that more often than not the first people to call someone a racist are racist themselves. Only a real racist can find racial undertones in cotton today or believe that the cotton industry still exists as a dagger to remind black Americans of a darker and more terrible time in our history.

I know what toxic masculinity looks like. It looks like keyboard warriors who take their jobs a little too seriously. It looks like cowards who pick on easy targets like a child. Who wish rape on a little girl. Who wish—anonymously, of course—a bullet in the back of my head. It looks like unintelligent individuals who have no real validation of their own principles (if they have any) taking their fear out on women and children.

What are they afraid of? They are afraid that I am right.

Toxic masculinity is a lack of real masculinity. We need real men in society who understand that. We need real women who promote it. We need parents who take their jobs seriously. The endless attack on manliness from all sides has to stop. The truth is, there has never been a better time to be a woman in America. That may make some people mad, but it's true. Today, women can vote. That wasn't always the case. Forty years ago, there were no two-income homes. Men worked out of the house; women kept the house. No more, no less. That doesn't apply today. Things have changed for women, and they have changed for the better.

TAKING ABUSE

Some people might think I'm emotionless and this kind of press coverage doesn't affect me. That's wrong: it sucked for me. It was hard. There are days of self-doubt, questioning who I am and what I'm doing: *Is this amount of hatred worth it? Why am I putting myself through this?*

Because here's the thing: There are people in the world who legitimately want me dead. We get death threats regularly. I have fans who know where my kids go to school, so I have to assume I have haters who know that, too. That is one of the reasons my kids don't go to public school anymore.

At the end of the day, nobody really likes to be hated. I've learned that it's one thing to stand for something you believe in when you're surrounded by a supportive circle of people. It's another thing to stand for something when it seems everybody hates you for it. You find out what you really believe in when you're standing by yourself.

I don't really care if I offend people, but I am careful with what I say about more sensitive topics, like suicide and sexual assault, for example. I'm not heedless about the power of my words to hurt or cause damage. To filter myself, I run my ideas through a couple of people, including my wife. For example, I'm not a racist person, so I don't want my words to be misconstrued as racist, and I'm not homophobic and don't want to come off that way. It's really important to me to check my thoughts and reactions with people I trust before I take them out into the world.

I don't care if I post something that people find offensive. I care if I do or say something wrong. If I'm not wrong, I'm posting it. If people get bent out of shape, that's on them. I'm just doing what I do.

I tell you all of this because I want you to know that standing up for what you believe in isn't always easy. In fact, most of time it is the hardest thing to do. I said what I said; I don't regret it. It was very hard on me and my family. It was hard to see people go after my kids. However, it wasn't for nothing. Things calmed down after a week or so, and life went on.

I pretty much forgot about the Gillette story until July 2019, when a report came out that Gillette's parent, Procter & Gamble, experienced a catastrophic loss in the six months after releasing the ad, taking an $8 billion write-down.

I felt a bit overwhelmed. I'm not so pompous as to say, "Look what I did," but I did have a sense that God was talking to me and showing me why I do what I do. I'm not claiming that I was solely responsible for the loss in profits, but it's ignorant to say I had nothing to do with it. Enough people saw what I had to say and agreed with me to make an impact.

With everyone else, I helped evoke a unified response of people coming together and saying, "This is garbage. We don't believe that. You attack us, we won't buy your stuff." There is a direct consequence to corporations pushing these kinds of false narratives, and we are not going to let them dictate who we are and what we do.

After the report, I did what anyone with a social media following would do. I started a live feed with my audience. I wanted them to know what had happened and that everything wasn't for nothing. I told them, "Sometimes, in this world that I'm in, and sometimes in this world that we all find ourselves in, we find ourselves asking questions about why we put ourselves through difficult things, why we make the choices we do, why decide to stand in our decisions. And here was the answer."

To me, the report was an example of why it's important to stand for what you believe in, even when it feels like the whole world is against you. Almost always, there's a silent majority of Americans who feel the same way I do. Just because they're not as vocal about their opinions, that doesn't mean they don't exist or aren't paying attention. This is the same silent majority that got Trump elected. This is why a picture of me and my kids that absolutely destroyed my family for a week turned out to be a valuable piece in the fight against the false narrative of toxic masculinity. That is also why you must stand and always fight, even when it seems like the world is against you.

CHAPTER 7

⸻

TATTOOS

"Do not cut your bodies for the dead or put tattoo marks on yourselves. I am the Lord."

—LEVITICUS 19:28

I'm sure that I am just like you. I'm sure that every person reading this with tattoos has heard that verse more times than they can count. I'm sure that there isn't much I could tell you that you already don't know about religion or the Bible. I have often found that the people who seem to have the biggest issues with "religion" or the "church" are often the most well-versed people within the text of the Bible that you will find.

Tattoos helped me see that.

I could sit here and write about context while reading the word of God and tell you that context is everything. It's funny how some things never change. In fact, context is even more important today than when the text on the pages that are read in churches every single day were first written. I have had many discussions with people about what I think the Bible means when it says certain things. But who in their right mind would say something like that Leviticus quotation today?

This is not a chapter about religious definitions or whether or not the texts of the Bible are literally true or whether or not human error can occur in translation. This is a chapter about tattoos and where they lead. Follow me down this road.

How could a person's tattoos make a difference or a change? Let's be honest. Unlike people, not all tattoos are created equal. I wonder what type of tattoos you have. Do they tell a story? Do they tell the world the story you want people to know about you? Why else do we put permanent things on our bodies if not to make a statement to everyone who will take the time to look? Maybe you are a tribal tattoo type of person. Pretty much everyone between the ages of thirty and forty-five has a tribal they would like to forget. Like many things, that was a trend that ran its course. It went from a cool thing to something to make fun of faster than most would like to admit.

Maybe you are a wording type of tattoo wearer. Nothing is easier than to tell your story by putting it into words on your body forever. Maybe your tattoos revere someone you love? Either a loved one who died in their time, or someone taken too soon…reverence all the same.

Even at thirty-three years old, and many tattoos later, I recall the fear I felt about my grandmother finding out about my first tattoo: the stereotypical barbed wire around my upper right bicep that was supposed to make me a rebel. The artist was named Cindy, and I remember the experience of getting it. From a very early age, I knew that I wanted full sleeves on both arms. I never had a desire for tattoos on any other location on my body. I don't know why I wanted tattoos. My grandparents have been adamantly against tattoos my *entire* life. I don't blame them. In their day, tattoos were associated with evil. They were reserved for people with no future or who had thrown their life away through bad decisions. This obviously was not true for everyone, but that was how they saw it.

Tattoos have been a part of society and culture for many years.

The military have been getting them for what seems like forever. Maybe that's where the real passion started. For longer than I care to guess, military service members have been their experiences in the service on their skin. Maybe it was to remember a fond memory like getting drunk with your brothers-in-arms on a duty station in another country—to always remember what you meant to each other. Or maybe it was to remember a fling, or a chance meeting the one who would become their spouse? (There is also taboo surrounding having the name of a lover tattooed on your body, but that's another conversation for another day.) Or maybe they tattoo their body and endure pain to remember a tragic loss. Maybe the tattoo isn't to remember the good times, but to remember the bad times. There is something about replacing pain with a different kind of pain.

We all have our reasons and our stories surrounding why we got a tattoo in the first place. So what was mine?

I suppose I thought it would help me get all the girls by showing how cool I was, and that pain didn't bother me. Maybe I wanted to show how "grown up" I was—I could do what I wanted with my now eighteen-year-old body. Maybe it was to show that I was a rebel, and a rule breaker who could not be tamed. Maybe, just maybe, I was hiding something. That tattoo was supposed to do a lot of things, but it didn't. In fact, I discovered that people found my first tattoo funny more than anything. I realized very quickly that you can't look for vindication in other people. Like many, I found that tattoos really only have weight, power, and authority to the people who actually got them in the first place.

I'd be lying if I didn't admit that I regret that first tattoo, which I later covered up with different art. (Word to the wise: Good tattoos are not cheap tattoos. Don't get a tattoo on a budget, you'll regret it. I did.)

My generation is the generation that broke the tattoo taboo. Until around 2005, people with visible tattoos were still labeled as troublemakers, bikers, or performers in rock bands.

I knew I wanted my arms to be filled out with tattoos. My tattoos tell a story of what's important to me. My right arm is the life arm, sharing some of the story of my life. That's where I have my kids' birthdays and the quote "pain is a liar." My left arm is the patriotic, military arm. I love that I have two different phases of my life represented on my body.

DON'T JUDGE A BOOK BY ITS COVER

Often, the people who seem to have the biggest issues with religion and the church are the most well-versed in the Bible. Ironic, isn't it?

The biggest video I ever made started with a comment someone made about my tattoos.

Throughout my social media journey, I have dealt with a lot of negative comments. People hate me and say horrible things about my family. As I explained in the last chapter, there actually are people out there who have told me they hope my daughter is raped and sodomized. It's horrible.

But of all those comments, the one that really set me off seems, at first glance, kind of inoffensive. It was a comment on my Twitter feed:

"Graham, I really love your message, but your tattoos make you look trashy and, as a Christian woman, I just can't stand to look at you."

I have no idea who this woman was. I imagine her as a middle-aged person. I still wonder if she knows that my response was to her. At least she was straight and to the point, right? Compared to the comments I received after the gun photo went viral, her comment seems like a walk in the park.

Yet that comment touched a deep, deep chord in my psyche.

For you to understand why I reacted the way I did—creating a video that ultimately reached almost half of America—you need to know a little bit more about my history. I want to take you back and tell you why I even am a Christian in the first place, and how hard that journey was.

Remember how I told you in chapter 2 that Pastor Darrell was going to play a big, unexpected role in my relationship with God? I couldn't tell you that story then, but now that you know more about me, I can. This is going to be a long detour—but it *will* come back to tattoos, I promise.

MY SO-CALLED CHRISTIAN PAST

As I wrote earlier, because of the home situation in which I found myself as a child, church became a place of escape for me. For the two-year period between the start of sophomore and the end of junior year, the First Assembly of God became my haven. My retreat. My refuge. My fortress. Unlike a lot of people, my personal relationship with God and Jesus was secondary. My primary reason for being at church at that time was to get away from home.

The heart and soul of my time at church was the Firestorm youth group's worship band. After begging to audition, I got the chance when the rhythm guitarist left the position. That audition was where I met Pastor Darrell. He would quickly become an incredibly important part of my life. Darrell was the youth pastor; he led the band; and he had a close relationship with the band members. He was strict, too. When I approached him he wasn't sure I was "Christian enough" to be in the band, but I had the chops and they needed a guitarist, so I was in.

I was an unusual kid at church—a teenager who showed up on his own, without his family. It was going to take me a while to prove that I belonged. And so I began what I now call my Year of Jesus.

A couple of months after I got the guitarist role, during the summer of my sophomore year, First Assembly of God competed in an event called Fine Arts Festival that included a competition between the best youth Christian bands in the country. Our band had already competed all over Mississippi. We were ready to compete in the national event until the bass player had an emergency and had to drop out. At first, we thought we couldn't go to the festival at all. Then Darrell turned to me and asked, "Graham, do you think that you could learn these bass parts and take over the bass for us to get to Fine Arts?"

Now playing bass was not my strong suit, but this was my chance— my shot to be accepted by the clique by helping the band get this thing we all wanted. Of course I could learn the bass parts.

I had a week to practice before we traveled to Albuquerque, New Mexico for the festival. We didn't just compete; in the end, we won the whole competition! That year, we earned the title of being the number one youth worship band in the country.

After that festival, my whole world changed. We traveled to Europe and played all across Germany, which was super exciting. More important, I became an accepted member of the group, which is what I most wanted. I felt like I had a family again. Every day, I was learning about God and reading the Bible. We were traveling the world to spread the Word.

Life was good.

A lot of young Christians only understand religion through their parents. Religion is a social obligation more than anything else. You may get baptized, but you don't really have a relationship with God. You're doing what you do to please your parents. You go through the motions. It's your parents' relationship with God, not yours. I think that's why a lot of people who are raised in the church "lose their way" as they grow up and then "come back to God" when they are older. The parental pressure has been enforcing a relationship with God, rather than mentoring one.

The way Pastor Darrell taught me about God was different from my parents' way. He became the father figure I didn't have. I thought to myself, "I finally got something here. I got a family; this guy is like a dad to me. He's a pastor, he's teaching me about God. I'm finally figuring out about God myself, rather than having to accept the God my parents have been pushing on me all this time."

In retrospect, I know that I was looking for acceptance from Darrell. The church was my escape from home. Even though I loved God, I cared less about Him and more about my relationships with this new family I was building around me, including Darrell.

My relationship with God and the church was kind of like a relationship with a favorite football team. You learn the history and the traditions of your team, and you stick with them through the ups and downs. If you think about it, you probably realize that you care less about the team and more about the experiences you have with other people who also care about the team. At the time, that's what my relationship with God was like. I cared more about the experiences I was having with the people around me than my relationship with God.

I was spending so much time at church, working in the band, that we should have been paid for the effort. On Monday nights, we practiced. On Tuesday nights, we traveled to play in different places. On Wednesday nights, we had service and played at church. On Thursday nights, we practiced again. Friday nights we had free. On Saturday nights, we played in another church. On Sunday, we had Bible study in the mornings and played in the evenings. It was a full-time job. That was my everything. It really began to feel like an obligation. No wonder that at school I was known as "the Christian guy."

REJECTION

During my junior year, things started to get more difficult at church. In fact, I began to see a different side of it entirely. Darrell became hostile towards me because I had a relationship with Terry. I listened to rock music—"devil music," as he called it. He accused me of *backsliding*—the same accusation I heard every single day at home. He asked me if Terry and I were kissing or holding hands. I would go to his office to be interrogated about my relationship. Now that I'm a father, I don't know how I'd feel if a youth pastor took my kid into their office to speak about his or her private life like that.

All I knew at the time was that everything was falling apart. By the time prom came around, Darrell was acting more hostile towards me than ever. He told me to come to Monday night band practice, and when I showed up, I was the only one there. Turns out he had given me an earlier arrival time because he wanted to see me alone. He sat me down and dropped a six-page contract in front of me.

"These are going to be the new standards to be able to continue to play in the worship band here!"

I read through the document with a rising sense of disbelief. It was full of rules, such as what to do if you had a girlfriend (and more important, what not to do), how you couldn't listen to secular music, Bible study obligations, on and on and on. I looked at Darrell and said, "I don't know if I want to sign this. This seems crazy, and it seems ridiculous to have to sign it."

"Well," he said, "this is what it means to be a Christian."

That encounter broke apart everything I thought I had learned about religion. Here was this person who I thought loved me, this person who I thought was a representation of Jesus, this person I had come to look upon as a father. He was a pastor, supposed to "love as Christ loves." Instead, he put a contract in front of me that said his love and affection were contingent upon my signing it.

For two years I had worked to get out of my situation at home, where everything about my relationship with my mother and stepfather was contingent upon how "Christian" they thought I was. I had worked hard to become part of the youth group and the worship band, because I believed that this church was a different, more accepting kind of religion. And now I was confronted with the reality that no, love and acceptance could and would be withheld from me here, too, by Pastor Darrell.

I began to get more and more furious. In that moment, I found myself angry with God because of what people were doing to me. "The balls on this guy!" I thought. Does he not know everything I have done? Everything I have sacrificed? Every single day is a burden, and I have given him and this church my everything! Now they are going to turn on me. You are going to be just like everyone else? You are only going to love me if I do exactly what you say, how you say it, or when you say it? *You can take this religion and shove it!*

When I look back now, I know that my primary relationship in the church should have been with God, not with people. But I didn't know that then. When Darrell started to become hostile toward me, when he began to criticize me and turn against me, I saw how shaky my foundation in Christianity was.

WHEN I LOOK BACK NOW, I KNOW THAT MY PRIMARY RELATIONSHIP IN THE CHURCH SHOULD HAVE BEEN WITH GOD, NOT WITH PEOPLE. BUT I DIDN'T KNOW THAT THEN. WHEN DARRELL STARTED TO BECOME HOSTILE TOWARD ME, WHEN HE BEGAN TO CRITICIZE ME AND TURN AGAINST ME, I SAW HOW SHAKY MY FOUNDATION IN CHRISTIANITY WAS.

It felt like the entire world was crashing down around me. My parents always had been disappointed in me. In fact, I am not sure there ever was a scenario in which I would have met their expectations. I had come to accept that. The church was supposed to be different. The church was supposed to represent God's love. The church was supposed to accept everyone. I was beginning to realize that it was all just a lie.

In the end, I didn't sign Darrell's contract. He told me that I would not be allowed in the worship band and discouraged me from coming to the youth group at all. He thought it would be bad "for appearances." So I quit going. I stopped going to church, which had been such a huge part of my life.

I lost my way.

Eventually in the coming months, as you already know, I would lose everything.

One night I saw Darrell in our local Mexican restaurant. I was eating alone. I know he saw me. Yet he just walked away.

I was forgotten. I was lost. I was a kid with nowhere to go. I was alone.

Does it surprise you that I found myself hating God and religion? I was so angry about everything. Not only was my life completely deteriorating at home, but the only refuge I had was gone as well. Every single person in that church turned their back on me. Nobody from First Assembly of God or the youth group called me, talked to me, or reached out in any way. In their eyes, I might as well have been a demon-possessed person that no one was allowed to be around. If I wasn't what the church thought I should be, then I wasn't good enough to even bother to acknowledge.

I was ejected from the youth group about a month before I ended up leaving Mississippi and being taken to Florida. The night that I left my house for the last time, my Aunt Lilly, granny, Terry, and I went to our favorite restaurant.

Darrell happened to be there, too. I went up to talk to him.

"I'm being taken out of my home and I'm going to Florida," I said.

I don't know what I wanted from him, but I wanted something. He just shrugged and walked off. It was like I was dead to him. I couldn't believe it. I thought, "I've given you two years of my life. I've been with you more than I've been with my own family. I just told you I've been taken from my home, and that's all you can do is walk away?"

THE TWIST

As the years went on, I heard rumors that Darrell wanted to take half of the congregation with him to form a new church called The Point. He did exactly that, and First Assembly hasn't been the same since. A while later, I heard rumors that Darrell was stepping down as pastor of his new church because he'd had an inappropriate relationship with one of the eighteen-year-olds. This is just a rumor, but it is what I heard. However, in 2016, twelve years after I left the church, I received a text with a link to a newspaper article from someone I knew. "You got to see this," the text said.

The article described a Kentucky sex sting operation that had caught a Mississippi business owner and pastor soliciting an underage boy who was actually an undercover cop posing as one online. And there in the article was a mug shot of Darrell.

It's difficult to describe how I felt in that moment. Picture the scene. I was alone in my office. I probably read the article 100 times, staring at the photo, scrolling through Facebook to see what people were saying, reading it again. I had just been confronted with evidence that the person who taught me everything about religion turned out to be the exact opposite of what a Christian is supposed to be.

This man had spent his whole life talking about how homosexuality is bad, it's the work of the devil, and that homosexuals are going to Hell. As far as he was concerned, *any* sex was bad. And here he is, busted in a sex sting operation for soliciting homosexual sex from a minor, staring at me from a newspaper.

Talk about a moment that crumbles your foundations...

I thought, "God, are you messing with me?"

I had not come back to religion yet. I would need years to come back to God. In fact, my pain and confusion around God and religion almost cost me everything, including my marriage. Job, wife, kids—you name it, I almost lost it all because I was mad at God. I was a victim of a "man-run" church, and what those men thought my relationship with God should be.

It would take me the first thirty years of my life to figure out it wasn't God who hurt me. It was people who hurt me.

Ellisa and I were having troubles, and I had not yet realized I needed to put God at the forefront of our marriage and recommit myself to a religious life. Everything I thought I knew about religion, everything that I had, at least at one point, accepted about religion, I had learned from Darrell. And there he was, still staring at me from an article about a sex sting operation.

I thought about all the interactions I'd had with Darrell. I thought about all the interactions other kids had had with him. Knowing what I know now, it scares me to think about the times that other youth members at the church went to stay at Darrell's house. Whether or not anything happened, I can't say, but it's not a good look either way.

I thought about the hundreds or potentially thousands of people he affected and wonder if he knew how hard he made it for people to amend their relationship with Christianity. Did he know how, through his actions, he destroyed the foundation of so many people's lives? Our actions have consequences, and they often affect more than just ourselves. Did he ever think about that? Did he know he was like a dad to me? Did he know how much he hurt me when he abandoned me when I needed someone? Did he know that it would take me years to come back to the church because of the actions he and the church took upon me? I don't know if I'll ever know the answer.

I ended up finding my way back to God because I realized I needed to relearn everything I thought was true. For the third time in my life, I had to rebuild my understanding of religion. I came to develop a personal relationship with God. I realized God is the God of love and mercy. Although I believe the Bible is very clear about some things, I strongly disagree with the interpretation of God as a drill sergeant who punishes you the second you do something wrong. I don't buy the fire-and-brimstone thing. I don't believe that God will smite you if you do something wrong.

Today, I may not agree from a religious point of view with someone who lives the LGBTQ life. However, we are Americans, and people are free to do whatever they want. I don't hate anybody or separate myself from them or act any better than those around me. In my version of Christianity, you don't hate those people. You don't separate yourself from those people. You don't act like you are better than those people.

Yet to this day, the Christian community is full of people who say, "Well, you ain't got Jesus like I got Jesus, so I cannot even associate with you because I can't backslide. I've achieved this higher level of Jesus than you. When you get up to where I am, then we can be friends."

TODAY, I MAY NOT AGREE FROM A RELIGIOUS POINT OF VIEW WITH SOMEONE WHO LIVES THE LGBTQ LIFE. HOWEVER, WE ARE AMERICANS, AND PEOPLE ARE FREE TO DO WHATEVER THEY WANT. I DON'T HATE ANYBODY OR SEPARATE MYSELF FROM THEM OR ACT ANY BETTER THAN THOSE AROUND ME. IN MY VERSION OF CHRISTIANITY, YOU DON'T HATE THOSE PEOPLE. YOU DON'T SEPARATE YOURSELF FROM THOSE PEOPLE. YOU DON'T ACT LIKE YOU ARE BETTER THAN THOSE PEOPLE.

Knowing what you know now about my history with the church, about the way my parents judged me, and the way Darrell judged me, and their failures and hypocrisies that I have witnessed, you have a little better sense of how I felt when I saw this comment on my Twitter feed on July 2, 2018:

> "Graham, I really love your message, but your tattoos make you look trashy and, as a Christian woman, I just can't stand to look at you."

As I said, it wasn't God who hurt me. It was people who hurt me. People who can make a comment like that.

That comment captured so much of my experience. Everything I had learned about religion was taught by one of the worst people I can imagine. I genuinely have no sympathy for people who would solicit a minor for sex. If you mess around with a kid, you're dead to me. In my eyes, that's one of the worst crimes that anyone can commit. And there that crime was, done by someone who told me I wasn't "Christian enough."

I am fed up with the pompous, outdated mentality that Christians are somehow better than other people simply because they're Christian. All those feelings, all that history, surfaced when I read that one Twitter comment.

MORE LOCKER ROOM BRILLIANCE

The video I made in response to that comment never should have happened. As a general rule of thumb, you shouldn't post one video right before another, because they can kill off each other's engagement, and we already had filmed and produced a Fourth of July video that would be launched on the third—think explosions, fireworks, and the epitome of patriotism.

On July 2, I was sitting in the gym when an overwhelming feeling came over me that I needed to address that woman's comment. The feeling pulled me out of the gym; I didn't even finish my workout. I drove down to a parking lot beside the navigation lock on the Tombigbee River, because there is never anybody there. I filmed a video in my car and edited it together. The video has a split screen; the right screen is me talking and the left screen is a picture of me and my family in which my tattoo is showing. I labeled the video, "Don't Judge a Book by Its Cover."

Up until that point, everyone who followed me assumed I was a Christian, but I had never really stepped out in faith. That day, something compelled me to go public with it. My message was very plain and straightforward. I pretty much said, "Wouldn't it be nice if Christians behaved the way Christians were supposed to behave? The God I have come to know has a lot more compassion and understanding than is represented in that comment." I talked about cliques in the Christian world, and pointed out that in John 3:16 it says, "For God so loved the world he gave his only begotten son, for whosoever believes in him shall not perish but have everlasting life." It does *not* say that God so loved the world he gave certain people Christian status to decide if other people were Christian enough.

I called my producer to give him a heads-up. I don't normally operate like this; we have a plan and a schedule. But I just felt called to get this video out. I uploaded the clip to my social media accounts, but I really didn't think it'd do anything.

Within the first hour after uploading, the video had 13,000 shares, which wasn't even close to my record. Some of my videos have had 70,000 shares in the first hour. Conventional wisdom is that the first hour is when you get your highest share rate. I thought it might top out at around 20k shares with a million views.

I don't know why, but after I saw the first hour's results, I decided to pray. "God, I don't know why I'm feeling this way, but if you can use this video for Your good, if you can use this video for somebody that needs it, I pray that You just let it go." That was it.

Then, the most miraculous thing happened with my tattoo video. After the first hour, it exploded. In the first twenty-four hours, we reached 30 million views. It was astronomical.

Up until that point, my record number of shares was 700,000 on a single video. The tattoo video ended up with 1.8 million shares and 130 million views. It reached almost half the American population. Clearly, a large number of people could connect with the hurt and frustration I was expressing.

To say I was shocked is an understatement. Not only did we get 130 million views, but we gained a million followers in a week. *A million people* wanted to know more about what I had to say.

Those numbers were further proof to me that this was a God thing, not a Graham thing. I'm a redneck from Mississippi. How could I possibly articulate anything for that many people to listen to without help? That was another full-circle moment for me. God is working even when we don't see that He is. He's there when we can't see him. There's a light even when we can't see it.

WHERE WE'RE SUPPOSED TO BE

Every single thing we go through in life is meant for a purpose. It is meant for a reason. Why would I go through everything I went through in my life? Nobody should lack a normal family life, but I sure did. Why? Why would everything collapse for me at home, and then collapse at church at the same time? Why would I almost lose my marriage because of my childhood angst and the breakdown of my relationship with God? Why would my relationship with God break down and then be built back up?

I believe all that happened for moments like the tattoo video.

If I didn't have all that pain, if I didn't have all those experiences, if I didn't see the bad parts of religion firsthand—not just hear about it, but see it—then I would not have been able to bring out of my soul the words that connected to so many people that day and that week in the tattoo video.

Because of an older woman talking negatively about my tattoos, because of everything I had been through up to that moment, millions of people across the country were exposed to my words about God and religion. Millions heard the words they needed to hear that God is a God of mercy. He loves us, and simply wants a relationship with us. God used my circumstances to serve His purpose through that video. Just because you find yourself in a bad spot now, just because you're not where you want to be right this second, that doesn't mean you're always going to be there. I'd argue that no matter where you are *you are exactly where you're supposed to be* at every moment. Every day prepares you for the next. So cherish where you are even if it's terrible. All it is doing is making you more qualified for the next chapter.

CHAPTER 8

CONSERVATIVES CAN'T BE CHRISTIANS?

The Founding Fathers truly had the right idea in separating church and state. What a lot of people don't understand is that their reasoning for doing that was the exact opposite of the reasoning that is used to defend that separation today.

Let's begin at the beginning. There was one, ultimate motivating factor behind the first settlers coming from Europe to the United States in the first place: religion.

The Pilgrims and other settlers came to the American colonies because the countries they left didn't have separation between church and state. These people were persecuted by the state for their religion. They weren't able to worship their God in the ways they wanted. For that very reason, when America broke away from

England as a free nation, the Americans who wrote the Declaration of Independence and the Constitution made sure church and state were separated so that the state could not establish or favor any religion. The ideas of freedom and free speech were born from the idea of freedom of religion.

Since then, Americans have celebrated freedoms such as freedom of speech and the principle of no taxation without representation, but freedom of religion is what started it all. That was the primary factor that had people coming over here in the first place.

When the Founding Fathers who wrote the Constitution chose to separate church and state, it was because they didn't want the government to dictate how people chose to honor their religion or what religion to practice. The Constitution said nothing about the church speaking the truth of biblical principles to influence politics. In fact, it was the exact opposite: they didn't want the government interfering in the church. *That's* what they were afraid of, because there had been a history of government interference and persecution.

In the past the government often consulted the church to make decisions. Christian thinking and ideas are found throughout the Constitution and other founding documents. After all, where do the concepts of life, liberty, the pursuit of happiness, and all men being created equal come from? That is not a worldly perspective. That is a Christian perspective.

WHERE IT ALL WENT WRONG

In my humble opinion, the moment we got this backwards and

things went wrong was when churches were formally exempted from having to pay any income or property taxes, a common practice that was made into federal law in 1894. Don't get me wrong; there was nothing wrong with the basic principle: churches aren't taxed so that they can use all their money for charitable church purposes. Why should people who are being obedient to God and donating their money to church then see the government take a portion of that money by taxing the church's income? That doesn't make any sense.

Churches and other nonprofit organizations avoid taxes under title 501(c)(3) in the IRS code. That law was intended to protect the church from state power by preventing the state from taxing charitable work. Yet it actually ended up putting a *muzzle* on the church, because it has been interpreted to mean that churches aren't permitted to take political positions. The number one consequence was that churches became dependent upon tax-exempt donations, which they get because of that law—because of the government. The second you become dependent on government-related money, the government controls you.

Any church that thinks they're the boss in this situation believes a lie. For as long as the government controls the church's money, the government is the boss, because they can influence everything a church says and does.

You may say to me, "That's not true, Graham. The church is a 501(c)(3) organization, so they don't have to give the government money." Exactly. That's *exactly* how the government controls them—because what the government gives, the government can take away.

If you want clear evidence that the government is trying to put a muzzle on the church, look at what Democratic presidential candidate Beto O'Rourke said during the Democratic debates. Beto O'Rourke promised that, if he becomes president, any church that does not perform and accept gay marriage will lose their 501(c)(3) tax-exempt status. Now try and argue that the church hasn't opened the hen house to the wolf of the government telling them what they can do, how they can do it, and what they can actually believe.

The government controls the church because it controls the money. Believe me, it's that simple. And this relationship has caused an even bigger breakdown within the church, Christians, and society.

Consider the most common problem people have with the church: they say it is disconnected from society and from people who are not saved.

The reason for this disconnection is that churches are *no longer allowed* to talk about what people are dealing with. The government says to churches and to their pastors, "You can't talk about things that we say are political, like abortion, LGBTQ rights, transgender people, immigration. You can't talk about whether Jesus would be a socialist, because then you're stepping into politics. If you step into politics, we're going to take your money."

This situation has been made worse by churches themselves, especially the growth of megachurches. I'm not saying megachurches are good or bad, but I do see a consequence of them. The bigger the church, the more satellite churches it has and the more money it takes to keep everything running. As a consequence, church leadership begins to operate under a business mindset instead of a relational mindset.

Most mega-pastors are business driven. From the outside, it seems like they care about spreading the word of God. To a certain extent, this is true, until spreading the word starts digging into people's bank accounts.

These pastors have more influence in a single social media post than the church has had for hundreds of years. So, what's the problem? The problem is that they are afraid of speaking up for the big issues in our society. Why? They're afraid of losing their tax-exempt status, which would mean losing members, money, and support from their congregation and community.

As Christians, our ultimate obligation is to speak what we know to be the truth. For example: abortion is murder. That's what Christians believe. However, when's the last time you heard a mega-pastor come out and explicitly say that abortion is wrong, and that life begins at conception? According to the Bible, the Lord says, "I breathe life into you. I knew you in the womb." Can you think of a time when a mega-pastor has openly come out and said those things?

If you can't, I don't blame you. It doesn't happen, which all comes back to the fact the government controls the money. The hard truth is the fact that churches take in millions of dollars a year and that has played a *pivotal role* in the eerie silence that penetrates society. Out of fear of losing money, churches cower and refuse to talk about the truths which are evident within the teachings of the Bible.

Carl Lentz, the pastor of Hillsong Church in New York, was asked about abortion on the show *The View*. In his answer, he said that Christians are not supposed to judge, which is technically true.

However, most churches think that not judging is the same as staying out of issues, when these are two separate things.

Trust me, Jesus never cared about anybody's feelings. In fact, Jesus was all about politics; he was the *number one politician* of his day. He lobbied for the truth, instead of going with whatever was trending politically, culturally, and societally. Jesus was never afraid to address issues in his society.

He was compassionate, but he wasn't afraid to speak the truth on every matter. He punched people in the mouth with his compassion all the time. Today's society lacks this crucial element of truth-telling. Now, churches have become too afraid to offend anybody. To avoid offense, and to avoid offending the government, they stay silent.

When President Trump showed up in the Carolinas after they were struck by a hurricane, he visited a church in which the pastor prayed for him at the service. The next day, that pastor had to send a letter to his congregation apologizing that he prayed for the president. The prayer was seen as a political act.

Excuse me?

As a Christian, I'm pretty confident that we're supposed to pray for *everybody*, which includes the worst people in the world. Even if you don't agree with Donald Trump at all, even if you think he's a bigoted racist, he's still the president and the head of state for our country. Shouldn't that be something we pray about? Anyone who says they are Christian but who refuses to pray for Donald Trump is not living Christian values. So who's really being Christian—the leftist or the conservative?

TRUST ME, JESUS NEVER CARED ABOUT ANYBODY'S FEELINGS. IN FACT, JESUS WAS ALL ABOUT POLITICS; HE WAS THE *NUMBER ONE POLITICIAN* OF HIS DAY. HE LOBBIED FOR THE TRUTH, INSTEAD OF GOING WITH WHATEVER WAS TRENDING POLITICALLY, CULTURALLY, AND SOCIETALLY. JESUS WAS NEVER AFRAID TO ADDRESS ISSUES IN HIS SOCIETY.

Let's put the pieces together so far. Government muzzles churches with the threat that they will tax them if they speak about political things. And as churches get bigger, they behave more like businesses and become more focused on getting and maintaining donations. These combine to keep churches from taking a stand on the issues that are most important in people's lives today.

The church is not, and has never been, about sticks and stones. You can talk truth without being hateful or judgmental. Christians have no place to judge because they don't have that kind of power or authority. Only God has that authority. However, as Christians, we have a responsibility to talk about what we know to be true.

If you claim to be a Christian, that means you have certain beliefs. The Bible is at the core of these beliefs; the Bible is the ultimate living document of truth. If you believe the teachings of the Bible, you categorically cannot support abortion, which includes supporting politicians who are pro-late term and up-to-birth abortions. However, if someone has an abortion, that doesn't automatically mean the church doesn't accept or love that person. It means the church prays that they get saved and are able to go to heaven.

So this is what it all comes down to: many people on the Left who think they know the Bible and know the church are convinced that conservatives can't be Christians. Their argument is that Christians would never stand for Trump. Since I came out vocally as a Christian, I have often heard it said to me that conservatives can't be Christians. Apparently, there's no way I can be Christian and support Donald Trump. I can't be Christian and tell a woman what she can do with her body. I can't be Christian and not want immigrants to be able to come and go as they please. I can't be Christian and not be a socialist.

Trust me, the list goes on. In 2019, I hear these things said to me *all the time*. Their argument is that these are un-Christian behaviors or positions. I say they are exactly Christian behaviors and causes, but our churches aren't speaking about them the way they should. If the church felt it could speak openly about these subjects, you would see that these are, indeed, Christian behaviors and positions.

Where is the church in these conversations? The lack of a statement from the church is making the Left feel like they're right, and conservatives like they're wrong. The Left says, "If you're right, wouldn't the church be coming to your defense? Wouldn't the church be saying, 'life begins at conception'?" In the Bible the Lord says, "I breathe life into you. I knew you in the womb." But the church is muzzled, as I've explained.

Ask yourself, who's really following the money there? Who's really following public opinion instead of God's? In my eyes, it's not the conservatives. It's the people saying conservatives can't be Christians.

FREEDOM

So many gave their lives for us to live in true freedom. It is our moral obligation to continue to fight for it and to preserve it. Freedom isn't free. It also can *never* be taken for granted.

CHAPTER 9

PATRIOTISM IS *NOT* RACISM

On the morning of September 11, 2001, I was a freshman in high school in my first-period Mississippi Studies class. The intercom buzzed to life and we heard our principal.

"Young people," he said (he always said "young people"), "I'm interrupting our scheduled class because something is going on that I feel is important for everybody to see. Turn on your classroom televisions."

Well, the cable TV in our classroom was broken, so our class just carried on. It wasn't until the second period, when I went to Coach Able's biology classroom, that I began to see what was happening in New York and Washington. As we watched, the second tower was hit.

"That wasn't an accident," Coach Able said.

At this point, even President Bush didn't understand that we were under attack.

His aide had not yet interrupted his classroom reading before a group of elementary school children. But looking back, I know that Coach Able understood in that moment.

Most teenagers are dumb, and I was no exception. As a freshman, I knew nothing about the military, the Guard, or the Reserve. I didn't know that Coach Able was a First Sergeant in an MP unit as a reservist.

As we watched the smoke and the people running around, we heard casualty estimates of perhaps 20,000 or 30,000 people. Then an on-air camera malfunction caused an audio blip that made a really funny noise. When my friends and I heard that noise, we burst out laughing. I know what you are thinking. *You laughed?* To this day, I'm embarrassed and ashamed about the reaction I had to one of the most horrific moments in American history.

Coach Able approached me. He looked me straight in the eye. "Do you have any idea what just happened? Not only have tens of thousands of people just died, our country is never going to be the same. This has just changed everything."

He didn't treat me like a child. He didn't call me a piece of disrespectful crap. For the first time in my life, another man looked at me as a man, and spoke to me as a man.

I'll never forget that.

In that moment of looking Coach Able in the eye, I realized

what love of country and love of freedom actually meant. I saw in his eyes that, as an adult and a service member, he understood what was going on. He understood what was at stake, for him personally, and for the country. Over the next couple of months, Coach Able and other teachers left the school because their military units were activated. The effect of the 9/11 attack was clear, even in our small school in the middle of Nowhere, Mississippi.

Coach Able was right. Everything did change, in big ways and small ways.

I enlisted in my senior year and went to war over what I had seen on the television that day. If I hadn't gone to war, I wouldn't have become a recruiter. I wouldn't have found myself at the corner of Pearman Dairy Road in Anderson, South Carolina run off the road by a little old lady who didn't know how to drive. I wouldn't have made my first video. You wouldn't be reading this book.

We are all where we are meant to be in this very moment.

SEPTEMBER 12

We all know that the aftershocks of that attack changed our lives in ways large and small. But those of us who are old enough to remember September 11, 2001 (and I recognize that there are kids graduating from high school or even college now who are too young to remember the time before), can also remember September 12. That's a day worth remembering, too.

On September 11, 2019, I posted this tweet:

The best way we could ever honor those lost on 9/11 is to live each day like September 12. There is no race, gender, or political side. In the end, the only thing that matters is each other. Americans first. Americans forever.

On September 12, we were Americans. None of the bull crap that we argue about day-to-day mattered anymore. We were *Americans*. On that day, it seemed that *every single person* in the world was flying an American flag.

I suppose about 5 percent of Americans didn't want to go to war, but the other 95 percent did. Whoever did this, we were coming to get them. Republican, Democrat, black, white, gay, straight, trans— it didn't matter. All that mattered in that moment was America. Because America had been attacked, we had all been attacked.

America is not some sort of Utopian *Leave It to Beaver* family TV show. America is like a big, dysfunctional family. Siblings here can hate each other and bicker constantly. But by God, nobody else had better come after your brother or your sister, or you'll come out swinging. That's how I view America.

There is nothing wrong, and everything right, with being pro-America. With being a patriot.

WHAT IS PATRIOTISM?

The word "patriotism" is being changed by Big Tech and the mainstream media. If you Google the word "patriot," the first result is for the New England Patriots (okay, I can understand that). Then you'll see the definition of patriot as "someone who loves his country." But then you'll see synonyms like "nationalist," "ultranationalist," "jingoist." Big Tech is adding these synonyms to the definition of "patriot" to make it seem like patriotism is a bad thing.

It's a short leap from there to the position that if you believe America is the greatest country in the world, you're a bigot and you are the problem. In fact, some people on the political Left will argue that America is a horrible place.

"Don't you know," they'll say, "what we've done as Americans? Don't you know that we had slavery for hundreds of years? Don't you know how terrible we've been? Don't you know that we have homeless people? Don't you know that we're leaving babies stranded at the border when all they want to do is come here and be free? Don't you know how horrible America is?"

When Donald Trump ran for president, his campaign slogan was "Make America Great Again." The Left asks, "Was America ever really great?"

Yes, America was great. America is great.

People who say America was never great are purposefully confusing the meaning between "great" and "perfect." Nobody ever claimed "great" to be the same as "perfect." America has never been, and will never be, perfect. Perfect is not something we can achieve, but it is something we can strive for.

There's a lot of work to do. For example, there are still racist people alive in America today, and they should be challenged in their racism. The fact that they exist doesn't mean the entire country is a racist and horrible place. Is America as a whole racist? No. You're an idiot if you condemn the entire country as racist.

America has a lot of stains on it. As a patriot, I can face that fact with honesty. Slavery is a stain we'll probably never get away from. But look at how far we've come. As a society, we've taken a grievance of inequality and collectively decided to change it. Don't forget that we've had a black president. Think about that for a moment. Can you imagine that Abraham Lincoln, the author of the Emancipation Proclamation, could ever have imagined that a black man would sit in his seat?

That's what we've accomplished, and it's because of our love of America. Patriotism is the belief in the idea of America. Americans are not perfect. We are not. The idea of America and what it could be, that is perfect.

Now we're never going to achieve that. Never. Perfection is impossible. Even if we can't achieve it in practice, the idea of millions of people coming together is amazing. Blacks, whites, polka-dots, gays, straights, Christians, atheists, Republicans, and Democrats, the people who worship trees and the people who worship God, all coming together in this idea of one people, that is amazing. We are different, but we are all Americans.

At the end of the day, America is an experiment, and coming together is what is necessary for this experiment to succeed. Nobody knew what was going to happen when this country was created. Nothing like it had ever been tried before. It shouldn't have happened. Heck, it shouldn't have worked.

The Constitution is the most perfect document humans have made in the history of the world. But it's not perfect—that's why there are amendments. Its near-perfect design allowed that to happen. The Founding Fathers who wrote it were not perfect—far from it. (Benjamin Franklin, for example, was a sex addict.)

Critics of America, people who question how I can be a patriot and not automatically also be a racist, say that because the Founding Fathers were not perfect, what they wrote was not perfect, so everything must be terrible. You can Monday-morning-quarterback the Founders and what they produced all you want, but what they did was better than anything that came before.

For the first time in the history of the world, a group of people came together because there was injustice and decided they were going to change it by creating their own country. Think about that—imagine trying to create your own country now. Then they decided to fight to defend their decision. Whether you believe the world is a few thousand years old or a few billion years old, this fact doesn't change: for the first time in the history of the world, a group of people who want to create something more fair and just actually win. A bunch of farmers and rednecks defeat the most sophisticated army in the world.

We don't have a king today, not only because the Americans won, but because our forefathers chose to do the exact opposite of what anyone had ever done. Instead of crowning King Washington, they decided to give power to the people. Their motto was, as ours still is, *E Pluribus Unum*—"out of many, one." The people decided who would rule, and they decided when an individual's rule was over. The individual states had power, separate and independent from the federal government. There would be three coequal branches of government that check and balance each other, so that no branch has ultimate authority.

This idea of America is genuinely as close to perfect as anything can be. To this day, many countries formulate their democracy around what America has done.

Ask yourself, what happened? Would the Founding Fathers be happy with the way we're talking to each other now? Are we confusing imperfection with failure? Are we blurring the lines between racism, bigotry, and patriotism? The answer is no they wouldn't, and yes we are!

Simply because we say we love this country and we love the idea of America, that does not mean we are saying everything in America is good.

We are saying we believe in America. That's what patriotism is.

Think back to September 12, 2001. That day, we all believed in America. If a great tragedy can bring us together, why can't we be equally patriotic and stand together every single other day?

CHAPTER 10

———

LIFE STARTS NOW

Baby lives matter. Let's just get that on the table.

What are the biggest divides and conversations in our country today?

Some people argue that it's immigration. Others say healthcare or gun rights. I like to look for the *root cause* of all our issues. For that reason, I believe that abortion is the single most important topic of discussion in our country.

Think about it: Why do we care about immigration? Why do we care about equality? Why do we care about racism, gun rights, and protecting children in schools?

We care about all of these issues because we believe that *life matters*. We believe the life of an individual has importance and is worth fighting for. If life didn't matter, why would we fight for equality and against racism, for example? Because life matters, we believe people deserve to be treated a certain way, with certain equalities and opportunities.

Would we do that if life *didn't* matter, if life *wasn't* important, if *personhood was something we could define*, rather than something we accepted for all persons? As soon as we begin defining personhood, as soon as we begin defining when life begins—and thus when guaranteed human rights, life, liberty, and the pursuit of happiness all begin—we've lost the battle for all the things we're fighting for.

You cannot separate valuing life from all these other things we debate and still be able to make a valid argument. The reason we fight so hard for our rights and freedoms is that we understand, in our chemical makeup, that life is the most valuable thing across the board. All the other important issues that stake a claim on our political careers, our faith, our understanding of how the world works, our traditions, and how we raise our families are based on valuing life above all, first and foremost.

Everything is centered around the fundamental idea that life is the most important principle, and that everything else springs from that.

WHERE WE WENT OFF TRACK

Our shared acceptance of this fact was undermined by the US Supreme Court's 1973 Roe v. Wade case. That decision legalized abortion, and I believe that's when things began to fall apart in our society. Admittedly, abortion is an uncomfortable subject to talk about. But we need to talk about it.

People who support abortion rights like to refer to the worst-case scenarios when they defend abortion. The three most common arguments for abortion are: to protect the health of the mother; because the baby might have something wrong with it; or if a woman was raped.

Let's get the first one out of the way. The only valid argument anyone could have for an abortion is that the mother would die if the pregnancy continued. You don't want to trade one life for another. Those situations are incredibly rare, especially with improvements in healthcare.

Abortion advocates point to the absolute worst scenario possible—rape—because those are the cases to which society reacts most strongly. Yes, it sounds horrible to be raped and then to carry the resulting baby to term. That sounds like a more compelling defense of the right to an abortion than, say, a situation in which a girl got pregnant with her boyfriend and they decided they didn't want to have a baby right now. Or you have a career and "now is not a good time." Or you got pregnant with somebody you met two nights ago. That doesn't sound like such a good argument by comparison, does it? It all boils down to selfishness.

The fact is, rape cases make up less than 1 percent of all abortion cases. Where else in society do we make a rule based on less than 1 percent? Nowhere.

Imagine two sonograms, side by side. One was conceived by a married couple. One was conceived by a rapist. How would you identify the rape baby? Can you pick? This one was conceived by two people who love each other. This one was conceived by two people who don't know each other. They have the same organs.

They each have ten fingers and toes. You can't say, "Oh, that first baby was conceived by two people who love each other, so that's a person. But the second baby was conceived by a rapist, so that's not a person." In other words, it's disposable.

How can one be deemed a person and the other not?

That doesn't make any sense at all. And it punishes an innocent child who had no choice in the matter.

When we start making these judgment calls about what's a person and what's not, we're selecting what criteria must be met to deem someone human. If we think about other examples where people did this throughout history, we get into dangerous territory. What happens when people say, "Your religion is wrong, so you're not a person"? Or, "Your skin color is wrong, so you're not a person"? Or, "Your mother and father didn't love each other, so you're not a person"? The Holocaust comes to mind. So does slavery. Throughout history, humans have dehumanized other humans based on their skin color or religion. Arguing for abortion is the exact same thing.

Let me bring in another horrifying thread here. When New York's legislature announced they'd allow up-until-birth abortions in certain situations, an entire community of people was shocked. I was sick at the thought; I couldn't process the idea of late-term abortions, let alone up-until-birth abortions. If you don't know what such an abortion entails, let me help you out. Doctors kill the baby inside the mother, but the mother still has to give birth to a dead baby.

How can anyone say that baby is not a person?

We need to think how we are defining personhood. Does person-hood mean a woman's water has to break so a baby can pass through her vagina? If so, are C-section babies any less than human? Do they have different rights to everyone else because they didn't pass through a vagina? I was born by C-section. Does that make me less of a person?

Or let's say the baby has Down's syndrome. Are you saying that baby is less of a person? I don't think that's a valid argument for an abortion. In the vast majority of cases, people are arguing for abortion or having abortions for selfish reasons.

The moment you start to peel the argument of defining personhood back, it becomes nothing but ridiculous. These days, babies are born in different ways. Many babies are delivered by C-section. Some women experience complications during pregnancy; their babies may be born two months early and have to sit in incubation chambers until they're ready for the outside world.

Let's talk simple truths.

The bottom line is that we *cannot define when a person is a person* because there are way too many loopholes and faulty foundations. The one argument I have found to be stable and defensible is that life begins at conception. That is the *only* argument that holds weight in the debate about personhood.

Find me a loophole there; I'm convinced there isn't one. You can't argue that the baby conceived by loving parents is a person and the one conceived in rape is not. You can't argue that the baby that didn't pass through a vagina isn't a person. It's ridiculous.

There is no other definition of the beginning of life than the moment of conception.

The second a baby is conceived, that person is protected and entitled to basic rights and freedoms. Nobody is arguing that you have to raise the kid; that's why we have adoption and foster care systems in this country. True, the foster care system has a lot of problems. But I'm pretty certain that no kid in foster care ever thought, "I wish my mother had aborted me." I wasn't in foster care, but I had a difficult childhood. I never once wished my mother had aborted me. People just don't think that way.

Life begins at conception. Yet some people are arguing for what amounts to infanticide. In a radio interview, the governor of Virginia, Ralph Northam, defended up-until-birth abortion by explaining that some babies survive abortion. The baby would be born, and the mother and doctor would have a conversation about what to do next: let the baby die, keep the baby, or put it up for adoption.

This is beyond me. If that baby survived an abortion, they're breathing. How can you possibly argue that isn't a person? To allow that baby to die is to commit the crime of murder. To commit infanticide.

I've lost count of the number of people who have wished that my daughter is raped when she turns thirteen years old so my family would have to face this choice. Although that's a terrible act to wish on someone, it's also a terrible reality that needs to be addressed. It is almost unbearable to imagine this as a father. The trauma, pain, and shame of an act that is supposed to bring joy would instead be a horrific event that removes power and choice from an individual. Dealing with that would be unimaginably difficult.

I know there is not a simple process of healing in these situations. I can only imagine what a world-shattering, life-changing event it would be. Yet, in all of that pain, I would hold her and comfort her as well as anyone possibly could. I would talk to her about the fact that she is carrying a living being that God created, and we do not have the authority or the power to define whether that's a person. It's not our job, not our right, not our purpose. I would tell her that if she was not able and willing to raise that child, we would help her find a loving family for her child. Most importantly, my wife and I would stand by her every step of the way.

Do you believe in civil rights? Every single civil rights argument you can think of falls apart if we accept that certain conditions must be met in order for someone to be considered a person, and thus to be sacred. The only reason arguments for civil rights exist is because of the basic understanding that life is sacred. The bottom line is that *every person's life is irreplaceable*. Every single person has the God-given right to life, liberty, and the pursuit of happiness.

As soon as we argue about meeting certain criteria to define personhood, we've lost the argument entirely, because then there is really no argument to have at all. A person is a person no matter how young or how small.

Now someone who still disagrees with me might argue that I'm not being morally consistent if I oppose abortion and support the death penalty, which is something many conservatives do. Those are two different things. With abortion, we're talking about a totally innocent life. With the death penalty, we're talking about the life of a person who has made a lot of bad decisions. The Bible is *very specific* about obeying the laws of the land.

DO YOU BELIEVE IN CIVIL RIGHTS? EVERY SINGLE CIVIL RIGHTS ARGUMENT YOU CAN THINK OF FALLS APART IF WE ACCEPT THAT CERTAIN CONDITIONS MUST BE MET IN ORDER FOR SOMEONE TO BE CONSIDERED A PERSON, AND THUS TO BE SACRED. THE ONLY REASON ARGUMENTS FOR CIVIL RIGHTS EXIST IS BECAUSE OF THE BASIC UNDERSTANDING THAT LIFE IS SACRED. THE BOTTOM LINE IS THAT *EVERY PERSON'S LIFE IS IRREPLACEABLE.* EVERY SINGLE PERSON HAS THE GOD-GIVEN RIGHT TO LIFE, LIBERTY, AND THE PURSUIT OF HAPPINESS.

No part of the Bible says being a Christian is easy. No part of the Bible excludes Christians from facing the consequences of their actions and decisions. For certain situations, I am pro-death penalty. If you commit mass murder, then the state is probably going to execute you. If you break into someone's house and get shot in the face, well, you made a series of really bad decisions, didn't you? There are consequences for your actions.

The abortion conversation does not even take place in the same realm as the death penalty conversation. To abort a baby is to abort a completely innocent person who has never had a chance to make a single decision, let alone a bad one. For the state to execute a mass murderer is to bring someone face-to-face with the earthly consequences of their own choices.

I strongly believe that murderers, rapists, and people on death row can find Jesus and get saved. And if you're truly Christian, then you will recognize that your life on this planet is just a blip on the radar, because your eternal soul goes to Heaven or Hell. In the grand scheme of things, we're talking eighty years here (if we're lucky), compared to an eternity somewhere else. This is hard for a lot of people to think about, because we're often focused on the now and our lives every second.

If you truly believe in God and Heaven, you're playing a much bigger chess game for eternity. God deals in matters of the soul, not the physical world.

And we are *not* God.

CHAPTER 11

────

DO YOU KNOW WHERE YOUR KIDS ARE?

In recent years I have had the privilege and honor to speak at major universities across the country. To think that a guy from Caledonia, Mississippi, with only a high school diploma would be at places like the University of Florida or Arizona State University is insane. Yet, that is where I find myself these days.

This privilege has opened my eyes even more to the fact that we are losing our children. We, as parents, only have a short time with our "babies." Hence the title of this chapter. Do you know where your kids are?

On November 13, 2019, I had the opportunity to join Charlie Kirk and Turning Point USA at the University of Florida. I had never been to the Swamp, but as a 'Bama fan my entire life, I had a firm hatred towards the Gators (I have experienced ten-plus years of heartbreak on account of the football rivalry between Florida and the Tide). Yet I must say, the campus was beautiful. The stadium was everything I imagined it would be, and the weather was as you would expect in a place called the Swamp.

As I prepared to speak in front of a packed theater of people eager to hear both Charlie's and my points of view, I began to notice exactly what was in store for us. This particular type of event was geared towards discussion. You hear it all the time that the left and the right only talk to people who are on their same side, so we figured that we would do the opposite. It is one thing to only have conversations with people who agree with you. It is a completely different thing to walk out on stage in front of people who don't agree, dislike, or even hate you for what you believe.

We decided to only allow questions from those who disagree with us. We wanted to have a dialogue with those that disagree, because how is progress supposed to be made if you only ever talk to the same people who agree with you, over and over again?

Of course, that meant there was going to be some hostility, too.

My early years growing up in Mississippi sheltered me a bit as to what is happening within our country. I will admit that things are simple in the South and we like it that way. We like to hold on to the ways of old. We like to believe in certain standards of moral understanding. It is simply the way that we are. The rest of the world isn't that way. I have learned this quickly and abruptly in the past three years.

As Ellisa and I approached the theater, we were escorted by a staff member through the back door, ensuring no one in the line saw us. This was for two reasons. First, many people would want to speak to us, take pictures, and so on. Although I love that, we simply didn't have that kind of time at this event. The other reason was because protestors were there in force—not only from the radical left side, but also the radical right. You heard me: I said the radical left and right.

Inside this theater was a heaviness like I have never felt before. We could feel a presence that did not want us there. We could feel the attacks against us for speaking what we know to be true to these young Americans.

I am not normally nervous before speaking. However, I could feel what everyone else was feeling. This one was different. This one meant a little more. This one was us against something dark. This one was a chance to stand firm in our resolve in front of a live audience, and in front of the world through social media.

On social media most people just see the viral videos. They see the perfect looking photos that photographers are paid a lot of money to capture. What you don't see is a group of individuals praying in a dressing room for the heart and soul of everyone in that building. What you don't see is how much we care and love everyone, even—especially!—because we felt that heaviness.

The next couple hours went by in an instant. Ninety-five percent of the attendees were college-aged. We opened the floor and took their questions for an hour. People were agitated, even aggressive.

What are your feelings on conservatives interacting with homosexuals?

Do you believe in real conservative values—that our Founding Fathers deemed America to be a white European nation?

Should all black people, Asians, Mexicans, Hispanics, and mixed-race people be kicked out of the country?

On and on it went. They were intense, to say the least!

There is so much anger and hurt within our society. There is so much confusion among our youth and they are just screaming to understand.

I heard everything from extreme socialistic viewpoints all the way to racist ones. From people who believe we as a country should accept anyone and everyone with no form of checks and balances. All the way to people that believe America was intended to be a White European nation and we should accept no one. The *real* things that are going on with our kids are very, very frightening.

How did we get here?

What happened?

Why are college campuses breeding grounds for the vast indoctrination of our youth into socialist ideas? Why do our children believe that they have "rights" to things like internet access, cell phones, a house? Why do they believe that if they were born one sex and want to be another, they have a "right" to change? Why do they believe they have a "right" to the material success their parents worked thirty years for? Why do our children go off to school only to become someone else?

THE MASS SEXUALIZATION OF CHILDREN

Mass sexualization in our society is not starting at college. It is starting much sooner. It is starting when we are supposed to be their parents!

The attack against our children has been happening for years. A good friend of mine once said that two things destroyed not only our families, but also our communities.

The first one? Garages.

Yes, garages. Once upon a time, most Americans couldn't afford attached, closed garages. Most people got off work around the same time, parked their cars on the curb, and walked across the lawn into their homes. This naturally led to people saying hi to one another, and then conversations would take place. Community would be formed simply because you parked your car on the street and chatted with your neighbors.

As I write this book, I am looking outside my window at four bikes scattered in the front yard, with a couple of swords and Barbie dolls. My children and a few kids from across the street are arguing over whether or not the pass was incomplete on the previous play. The sad part? This is now a rare thing to see in America.

What's the second thing that destroyed our families? That answer probably also will seem strange to you: TV dinners. That's right— TV dinners. What did we do before TV dinners? We used to have a set dinner time. We used to have an understanding as families that dinner time was a sacred time set aside for enjoying family. We understood that that time was vital for remaining active in each other's busy lives. Then came the TV dinner. Now, instead of gathering around the dinner table, we gather around the TV. We let the TV talk to us, instead of talking to each other. Slowly but surely, that family connection was lost.

I am not so dumb as to sit here and say that garages and TV dinners explain everything. In fact, they are examples of a long line of changes that have led to the breakdown of our homes. So many families now have two working parents. They drop their kids into the system in preschool, maybe when they're only three years old. Those kids are forced to learn about HIV, AIDS, and sex. They're told, "You can be your own person. You can be whatever gender you want to be. You can do whatever you want to do. You can say whatever you want to say. You are entitled to anything you want."

There are no lines of respect anymore, no sense that they have to earn things. Parents fall into the trap of trying to keep the peace, of wanting to be their kids' friends, of not wanting to be the bad guy. They want to hang in there until they send the kids to college, and college can finish the indoctrination off.

You see, it is *our* job as parents to be parents! The system is designed for parents to simply insert a child into the "process" and then let the process raise the child while the parents simply keep the child from straying too far out of line. Until that child gets to college and then the indoctrination can be finished off.

Don't believe me? In the fall of 2019, we enrolled my daughter in kindergarten. The first form we were asked to fill out was not allergy information. It wasn't an emergency contact form. It wasn't even about lunch. Nope—the very first form we were asked to sign was whether or not the school would be allowed to include her in the HIV and AIDS education!

I am not the smartest man, so perhaps I am missing something here. Someone, please inform me if there is any reason under the sun that a six-year-old needs HIV and AIDS education. The simple answer is, there isn't one!

Do you have any idea what schools are teaching your kids? I will tell you that you probably don't. Most parents don't want to hear this, but it's true.

The society that we live in today is very sad. We live in a culture in which being a parent simply means being a friend. We live in a society that would rather offer children options than rules and standards. We live in a society that pushes "woke" agendas on our children so we feel better about our own insecurities. After all, Hollywood actors have three-year-old children telling them that they were born the wrong gender and want to change. Why shouldn't we just be our children's friends? It's so much easier than taking on the responsibilities of a parent.

We like to believe that we are doing right by our kids. We like to believe that protecting them from bad things is great. It is, and it isn't. True, it is our job as parents to protect. But it is also our job to teach! How are we setting our kids up for the real world if we are too busy telling them that they are great at *everything* they do? We tell them they can be whatever they want with no boundaries of any kind. (You parents know who you are!) The internet is full of videos of "singers" who were told they were great their entire lives, only to get on American Idol or the Voice and learn very quickly that's not to be the case.

BE PARENTS. YOUR KIDS WILL THANK YOU WHEN THEY HAVE KIDS OF THEIR OWN.

Real parents need to *step up*! We don't need to be friends for our kids. They will make friends on their own. We need parents to teach our future generation how to be firm in their convictions. We need parents to equip our children to believe in God, not to falter the first time they meet a liberal arts professor in college who tells them God isn't real.

I read an article that says by the age of ten, parents are no longer the main center of influence for their children. Their peers are. If I may be real for a moment, let me say that there are a lot of dumb ten-year-old kids walking around. I don't want them dictating how my children are going to be. And I don't like that schools can't punish kids any longer. I don't want my kids to grow up where there are no consequences for their actions. I want my kids to work hard for what they want and earn something. I want them to understand that everyone can't be everything. Everyone has their own strengths and their own weaknesses and that's OK! It is our differences that force us to form community and rely on each other. It is our differences that make us all the strongest together!

However, in today's culture we are teaching our kids the exact opposite. We are teaching them that they need no one. They don't need to believe in anything. They don't have to follow any rules because every rule was written by someone who doesn't understand what they are going through, so they don't have to listen. We need to teach kids that social media isn't real and what they see on CNN and other mainstream media sources are lies. We need to teach our kids to think for themselves. We need to teach our kids to believe in something!

That starts in the home. That starts with me. That starts with you. It starts with the family. It starts at the dinner table with conversations as a family. It starts with being a parent first, friend second. As a parent, I plead with you: do not let your kids be taught by others. Let them learn new things from experiences, sure, but form their convictions, morals, and beliefs in your home.

Do you know where your kids are?

It's a very real and terrifying question. Because if you don't know, I guarantee that everything that you don't want near your children does know exactly where they are.

Be parents. Your kids will thank you when they have kids of their own.

CHAPTER 12

GUN RIGHTS ARE HUMAN RIGHTS

The second biggest argument in our culture now is gun rights.

The attack on the Second Amendment is nothing new, but it has taken a more dangerous turn recently. Look at any Democratic politician on the podium right now. Every single one of them is fighting for some type of gun legislation. Failed presidential candidates like Beto O'Rourke are taking the argument as far as they can go. In a presidential debate, O'Rourke said, "Hell yeah, we're going to take your AR-15. If it's a weapon designed to kill people on the battlefield, we're going to buy it back."

The real issue isn't about banning AR-15s. It's about banning guns in general.

When the Columbine school attack happened, I was just a child, but I do remember the world watching in horror. I was too young to fully grasp everything that was going on, but I remember it.

Columbine was our first glimpse into how societal change in our culture was amplified by social media and 24/7 news coverage. Since that moment, we have been looking at life through the highlight reels of Instagram and Facebook.

In today's society, humans are more connected technologically than we've been before, and yet people feel more alone than ever. This means the conversation about guns has to be a conversation about mental health.

In the past several years, America has faced shootings in Las Vegas, Charlottesville, Broward County and Orlando, Florida, Dayton, and El Paso, to name a few. You have to ask yourself, what's going on? What's really happening? Is our society being taken over by crazy white supremacist nationalists wielding AR-15s who hate immigrants and people of color and who want to commit mass murder? We are led to believe regular citizens can't safely walk down the street, go to Walmart, or visit a hospital.

IT'S NOT ABOUT THE TECHNOLOGY

A few years ago, I was on FOX News talking about the Second Amendment, and I made a prediction. I was responding to a common argument, which goes like this: "Surely the Founding Fathers were only talking about muskets. Surely they never could have imagined the destructive power and capabilities of today's weapons."

I called that an ignorant argument. "If we're going to accept that mindset," I said, "and we allow the government to come after our Second Amendment rights because the technology was unimaginable then, what's to keep them from coming after our First Amendment rights? Because today's communications technology must have been unimaginable, too. The Founding Fathers never would have imagined that one person could say something into their phone and reach millions of people. They never would have imagined the internet, or blogs, or vlogs, Facebook, Twitter, or Instagram."

Many argue that free speech is the most important amendment, because humans should be able to say whatever they want to say, however they want to say it. We should be able to start conversations, arguments, and dialogue whenever we want.

So, what about when the government says we can't do that anymore? Don't tell me it doesn't happen. The very reason America was founded in the first place was because the early settlers weren't allowed to say what they wanted to say in Europe. They weren't allowed to practice religion the way they wanted to practice it.

History is riddled with examples of governments deciding what individual people are allowed to do and to say.

Think about it: which amendment is the most important amendment? In my mind, the Second Amendment is *the most important right* we have, more important than freedom of religion, free speech, pleading the Fifth, etc. If push comes to shove, the Second Amendment is the only amendment that fully insures the others.

LET'S TALK NUMBERS

Beto O'Rourke and other Democratic presidential hopefuls claim that they'll take guns away from American people if they don't hand them in themselves. That is a direct infringement upon our Second Amendment rights. Granted, Beto O'Rourke is not going to win the presidency, but he's not making things up. He's not a visionary or even that smart. He's simply regurgitating the information he hears behind closed doors. You hear similar things from Bernie Sanders, Elizabeth Warren, Kamala Harris, and every other person on the far Left who wants to go after guns.

All of them speak in similar ways. They cite 40,000 deaths due to gun violence in 2018. Such a statistic is used to incite fear in people. These politicians want the public to believe that 40,000 people died going to work or church or when buying a TV from Walmart. By phrasing their argument that way, they're intentionally manipulating information.

Yes, 40,000 people died from guns in 2018. But, remember, context is everything. The large majority of those deaths—60 percent— were the result of suicide, which is the tenth leading cause of death in our society right now.

The number of deaths due to mass shooters is as few as 172 that match the mass shooting criteria. Don't get me wrong; I believe that one death is too many. However, out of 350 million people, with five million registered gun owners in the NRA ALONE and likely more than one gun per family (I have about twenty guns myself), 172 shootings is not a situation that seems out of control.

Yes, twenty-two people died in a mass shooting in El Paso, which was horrible. However, the same weekend a year earlier, seventy-six people were shot in Chicago in gang-related violence with pistols and handguns. A month after the El Paso shooting, a single man in California stabbed four people to death. Where's the outrage about that?

A mass shooting is commonly defined as an incident in which four or more people are shot. By that logic, the incident in California could be viewed as a mass stabbing. In fact, statistically more people die from blunt object attacks. Should we get rid of hammers, too? Can we no longer own hammers without a permit?

Gun violence is horrible. My point is that you are hearing a fabricated lie when you hear that there is a horrible mass gun violence epidemic in society. Mass gun violence isn't as extreme as it seems. We see when a mass shooting takes place because it's plastered all over the media. Suddenly, we believe that the world is ending, and our children aren't safe.

MENTAL HEALTH IS THE ISSUE

If the majority of gun-related deaths are the result of suicide, I'm sorry to say we don't have a gun problem in the country. We have a mental health problem.

In the grand scheme of things, this is a great time to be alive. Think about it. A guy in his truck with nothing but a phone can reach billions of people, and he can also create a business with employees, providing a living for multiple families.

In a society where we are more connected than ever before, people are more alone than they have ever been.

We have to ask ourselves *why* people are committing suicide in the first place. What do they want to accomplish?

The Netflix series *THIRTEEN REASONS WHY* was one of the most watched TV shows on the streaming service when it launched in 2017. Bullying and methods of suicide feature prominently in it. The narrative is that suicide is the ultimate way to be heard, to respond to all the pain that a teenager or young adult has to deal with. By promoting shows like *THIRTEEN REASONS WHY*, we're pushing our younger generation to believe that suicide is the answer.

Tell me, where is the outrage about this narrative that Netflix is promoting to our younger generation, making them think suicide is an answer and a route they should explore? Where are the people marching in the streets against Netflix, or even against mental illness?

We are teaching kids that suicide is the best way to be heard. Or the best way to get back at people who have wronged you. Most of all, we are teaching people to believe the lies inside their own heads. We are teaching them that it is correct to believe the world would be better off without them. It is not correct!

Many people today struggle to find value in their life. I believe social media has a lot to do with this. People look at "famous" people on the internet, see all of the comments and the likes, and think to themselves, "Why can't I be like that? Why do I suck? Why am I not able to be popular like they are?" They don't realize that these images are lies, because they do not tell the entire story.

Take my life for example. You see my trips to New York or Washington and think, "Man, Graham gets to do everything!" What you don't see is the empty hotel room. What you don't see is missing my kids' football practices. What you don't see is the desperate need I have for someone to know the *real* me and not the "famous" me. What you don't see is the truth that being "popular" means that you actually are very alone.

One of the most frequent questions I hear is, "I want to be famous—how do I prepare to have a life like yours?"

My answer, "Get ready to be alone!"

What is really important is the little things. The moments that many would deem "uneventful" actually hold the most weight within our lives. In the same way that my parents forgot what living felt like because they were so heavily medicated, we are forgetting that real life doesn't consist of nonstop likes and views on social media platforms. We are not teaching that life, *real life*, is actually very hard at times. However, *it is worth it!* Every single person can find worth in their lives simply by looking into the faces of the people who care about them.

We need to get back to teaching everyone that our lives have value… so fight for it! Suicide is not a way to make your point be heard. Life is worth fighting for—you can find meaning by looking into the faces of people who care about you.

No, people are outraged by inanimate objects. A gun is an inanimate object. It does not get up and shoot people on its own. At the end of the day, the person who pulls the trigger is the problem.

If we lived in a Utopian society, we might be able to remove guns and get rid of the problem. But we don't, and we can't. Just look at drugs. Drugs are illegal, but that doesn't stop anybody from selling and doing them. Increased gun laws are only going to stop law-abiding citizens from owning guns. Criminals will kill people with or without gun laws. They will have all the guns because they do not care about gun laws.

THE REASON FOR THE SECOND AMENDMENT

The fact of the matter is that people don't want to hear the truth, which is that guns will kill people no matter what. Of course, we can do our best to limit and reduce the number of gun-related deaths, but we can't stop bad people from doing bad things if they want to do them badly enough. There's nothing that can be done to entirely end that. Evil people are going to do evil things.

IF WE LOSE IT, WE WILL NEVER GET IT BACK.

The real question is, why would we want to put good people, who care about their families, property, and individual lives, in a worse position to fight against evil people? Why would we want to tie one hand behind their back by taking away their weapon? Believe me, if someone has a gun and you don't, you're losing that fight. There is no fifty-fifty shot. There is a zero percent chance you are going to get out of that, because you are not going to win. That is the basis of the Second Amendment.

People tend to forget why the Second Amendment was ever created in the first place. It all started with a group of people who understood exactly what it meant for a government to not have the best interests of the people in mind anymore. They knew exactly what it was like to live in an environment in which they didn't have the means to fight for what they knew was right.

The Second Amendment is not just for hunting, or to run speed drills, see how fast you can draw, and how tight your grip is. That's lots of fun, but it's not what the amendment is for. Some people don't like to talk about this, because they are afraid they will be called conspiracy theorists, but the Second Amendment was put in place as a last resort. If the day ever came that the government forgot that the will of the people was its primary interest, the Second Amendment ensured that the people would have the power and opportunity to enforce their will back upon the government. That's the whole point of the American Dream in the first place.

If the government ever forgets its place, the Second Amendment exists to protect the people. Gun rights truly are human rights.

Gun rights are the only rights which ensure all of the other rights we have, across the board. If we ever give any of our basic freedoms away, we'll never get them back. As Americans, not only do we have a moral obligation to ensure the Second Amendment, but we have a responsibility to teach, educate, and train our future generations on the importance of protecting that amendment.

If we lose it, we will never get it back.

FOREVER

America is not done. God is not done. And God is not done with me yet. We are all unfinished. We're just getting started.

CHAPTER 13

OUR RIGHTS AND OUR FREEDOMS ARE *NOT* UP FOR DEBATE

If you've found your way through this entire book, you either love me or you hate me. I have learned that there really is no other way around it.

That's okay. In fact, that's the entire point.

I strongly believe that people should be able to have open discussions about their disagreements. It does me no good to try and make you feel how I feel. To try and make you understand my worldview exactly as I understand it is assuming that we all started from the exact same place. That is the very definition of entitlement.

We are not the same. Of course, in the sense that no person is better than another, we are all equal. Yet, we all have different lives, experiences, and interpretations of those experiences.

My story is not your story. Your story is not mine. Maybe you had a picture-perfect family life, or maybe you envy my childhood because yours was far worse.

By telling you who I am, I hope I have given you a better understanding of *why* I do what I do. Why I say these things in the first place. Why it is so vitally important for me to talk about them.

I am not ashamed of my life. I don't look back at my childhood and say, "Woe is me." That is the typical response in our current society and it's something that needs to be stopped. The world doesn't care about your hardships. They claim to on TV and motivational Instagram posts, but people really only care what you can do for them in the moment.

Instead, I look back and realize that what happened to me was exactly what was supposed to happen. Our society could use a little bit more of that thinking and a little bit less victimhood mentality. If anything had happened differently, I wouldn't be where I am today. Good or bad, we have to take what life gives us and use it to our advantage. We do not need more victims. We need victors!

Our history as Americans has led us to pivotal moments. Think about some of the most vital moments in American history, from the Revolutionary War to the Civil War to 9/11. All of these moments had one purpose: No matter the circumstance, we transformed it into the betterment of the American people. We could have felt bad for ourselves. We didn't. We made something of those moments.

The Revolutionary War was fought to establish something nobody had established before. The Civil War was fought to acknowledge the fact that every citizen deserved equal rights. Even 9/11, as horrible as it was, reminded us that, as Americans, we're all in this fight together. If somebody picks on one of us, they pick on all of us.

On November 8, 2016, something different happened with America. The question in the presidential election was no longer about the betterment of the American people. The challenge wasn't about making America better. It was about saving America from itself. If the conservative party had lost, I feel the American experiment, at least as we know it, would have been over. That fear was the underlying force driving a silent majority to the polls.

Modern society often falls into the mindset of victimhood. Somewhere along the way, we forgot what it means to stand up as Americans. Today, it feels popular to be the victim. It's popular to be helpless. It's popular to expect somebody to save us. This is a trap.

Everything starts at home. In this book I've drawn connections from the breakdown of the family, to the importance of commitments, to how we view relationships, to toxic masculinity (which is an utter attack on the family). By now I hope you can see that all our problems start from home and spawns out of selfishness. Every solution starts with an act of selflessness. It starts with giving more of yourself to your spouse, to your kids, to your job, to a friend, to your country. Worry about something or someone other than yourself. Trust me, it's an amazing place to be. It starts with training our kids to be actual adults and patriotic Americans who understand what that means, not what Big Tech says it means by altering the definition.

But that's not happening as much as it should.

We find ourselves in the situation we are in for three reasons:

1. A lack of faith in and acknowledgment of God in our society
2. The breakdown of the family
3. Entitlement, selfishness, and victimhood mentalities run rampant

Every single issue we face in American society can be broken down to these essentials. From failures at the smallest scale, of the individual and the family, we can see how problems grow to the largest scale.

Start with faith. As a Christian, I believe passionately that we lack an appropriate acknowledgment of the role of God in our society. Whether you are a Christian or not, it is vital for you to have faith in something! Atheism is extremely dangerous and not just for religious reasons. If you don't believe in anything, you have no moral compass to judge from. Without a moral compass, how can you be trusted to decide between right and wrong? A lack of belief is a dangerous mindset for living your life.

Another dangerous mindset: In today's society, we're told that our differences are not strengths, and that we are weak if we are not the same. You can see this with the "men are girls" and "girls are men" arguments: *Men can have periods and give birth, too.* The simple answer to this is obviously no, they can't. Yet we no longer accept our differences and our strengths that make us stronger together. We want to blur the lines of togetherness within our society and say we can do it all on our own. We can be whatever we want, and we need no one.

Americans aren't supposed to be the same. We're *supposed to be different*. The point of the American experiment is for us to relish our differences. Some people are weaker in certain areas where others are stronger. Those differences are necessary.

Another fundamental problem is we're forgetting to teach our children how difficult commitment is. *Real commitment is choosing every day, even when you don't 'feel' like it.* You're probably not going to accomplish everything you want in life, because you just can't be the best at everything. You're human; you're allowed to suck at some things. Figure out the things you don't suck at and focus on those. Work hard every single day. Realize that you probably won't make six figures a year straight out of college, especially with a liberal arts degree. That's just not how the world works. You're not going to make or have what your parents do right off the bat because they worked for thirty years to get there. You need to *earn* that.

We're failing our younger generations by not teaching them what it actually means to be American. We aren't reinforcing the fact that our rights and freedoms are *not up for debate*. One million three hundred thousand veterans have shed their lives to ensure those rights and freedoms for us.

Beginning with the Revolutionary War, we have fought and bled for these rights and freedoms as all of us Americans worked to make America better—not perfect, but always better. We do not give those up. Do we still need each and every one of those rights and freedoms, including an unfettered Second Amendment? The answer is unequivocally yes. This is not something we negotiate.

America is not a mistake. If America is a mistake, we're all mistakes, which leads us to the largest question of all: What is life? How do we define it? When does it start? If we don't understand that it begins at the beginning, all our other arguments for rights and freedoms crumble.

If we forget the most basic principles of what it means to be Americans, if we no longer have faith in anything, if we no longer value family or commitment, then we have moved to a place where our rights no longer matter and our freedoms no longer matter. We have moved to a place where we want others to take care of us and even to the sacrilege of determining who is worthy of being deemed a person.

If that happens, what's the point? Why is there even an America in the first place? Why are you reading this book?

You're reading this book because you believe in something. Maybe your beliefs are the opposite of mine; that's fine. We don't all have to believe in the same thing, but we do all have to believe in something. Belief in God. Belief in America. Belief in our families. Belief in ourselves.

Without belief and without hope, then all of this is meaningless.

On November 8, 2016, we were fighting for America. We were fighting for our futures and our kids. If Hillary Clinton had won the election, we would live in a very different world than we do today.

Now, the battle is just as big, if not bigger. Right now, we're in a fight for our country. As the generation in charge, we have an obligation to stand up and make our voices heard. Now is not the time to duck our heads, go to work, and pretend everything will be fine.

The Left has always been the most vocal when trying to influence the younger generation. It's time for us to realize that the younger generation is our future. It's time for the conservative people and Christians to stand up and be heard.

Let America 3:16 be our motto, to remind us of what America was supposed to stand for in the first place. America was an experiment under the divine, secure hand of God: The many are more important than the one!

Somewhere along the way, we allowed a small percentage of the population to make decisions for all of us. This is the exact opposite of the American experiment. Our obligation as Americans is to remember what it actually means to *be* American. Our job is to teach and always remind future generations how blessed we are to be Americans! We must teach them to never let that love of country go! Never give up our freedoms! Never give up our love for each other as Americans!

Choose to be an American, not a selfish victim who only wants what the country and others can give you!

It's time to be *real* Americans!

If you've read every word of this book and you're still here, you either love me or you hate me.

If you don't hate me then that can only mean one thing. Either

you're just like me or I'm just like you. Either way, we are the same…
Americans!

Are you still here?

Good.

Now let's get started, because we've got work to do.

ABOUT THE AUTHOR

GRAHAM ALLEN is a twelve-year Army veteran from rural Mississippi and a thirty-three-year-old entrepreneur, known as one of the Top 50 conservative voices in America. He is the owner of the media properties The Daily Rants, Rant Nation, and Dear America. Graham is responsible for building one of the fastest-grown digital social media audiences in America. In three years, he achieved 2 billion worldwide views on his combined platform. He frequently travels the country as a public speaker.

Graham hosts the *Rant Nation* TV show and *Dear America*, one of the fastest growing podcasts in the country. In 2017 the Huffington Post identified him as one of "22 Veterans to Watch." According to *The New York Times* and other sources, Graham had one of the top 100 most engaged Facebook pages in the world in 2018.

Make sure you aren't missing out. You can also reach out to him through America316.com.